Inducing Consciousness on the Way to Cognition

By

Glen Davidson

ISBN: 0-75967-098-6

This book is printed on acid free paper.

1stBooks - rev. 09/20/01

Contents

vi

Introduction

The interest in consciousness today is great, yet it is probably no more than the interest in the unconscious in the late nineteenth century and early part of the twentieth century. Jung, Freud, and Nietzsche found the unconscious to be key to much that is conscious, and that consciousness often plays a subsidiary role to the interests of the unconscious. This brings up the question of why consciousness is considered to be so important, and whether or not it should be thought so.

Probably the increased focus on consciousness today is partly due to the fact that while the unconscious can reach the conscious—and it can be studied, researched, and categorized—it cannot be considered as much more than an inferred realm psychologically and philosophically. At least this is the case for most people in modern civilization. So in our society today (and for the most part in others), the mysterious experiences of both the unconscious and the conscious are known in the phenomena of consciousness.

Then too, the unconscious tends to be assumed as explained adequately enough within the framework in which we can know it to exist. That is, it has been modeled and described, so that there seems little left to consider in ways other than via psychological, cognitive, and sociological models, for a non-exhaustive list. The mystery of consciousness remains, and if the unconscious affects it and is affected by it, arguably the conscious phenomena through which we primarily know about the unconscious have an inevitable *epistemological* priority in the mystery of existence as we experience it.

In this time of minutely divided and exponentially expanding knowledge it is this one thing that remains largely untouched by explanation. And this property of consciousness is a crucial part of the entire basis for all knowing and experiencing, the one through which the other parts of cognition are known. Consciousness is, however, a phenomenon with which we in fact deal rather successfully, at least by its own standards, while its most basic, intrinsic meaning seems to have eluded us—as does the knowledge of whether or not it has any basic meaning. It could be, for instance, simply incidental to meaning. Finally, if we would understand the world as well as possible, which might be useful for some knowledge, we must take into account the manner in which the objective world arises in the conscious mind.

Possible origins of consciousness are bandied about today, from Daniel Dennett's reflexivity, to quantum mechanics, and yet again to various neural correlates of consciousness. A good many useful discussions arise around the several postulated reasons for consciousness, even if they typically illuminate other subjects rather more than consciousness. One reason for the usual misses is that the "consciousness" being considered by the many is so unlike that considered by Nietzsche, Freud, and Jung. Free will, for example, is one of the aspects for which several quantum mechanists try to find an explanation. From sociology and psychology it appears that this is one of the least likely properties to exist as an appreciable factor in the consciousness of the herd. That is to say, social consciousness seems to be poorly characterized in terms of free will.

On the other hand, any explanation of consciousness must account for the ready appearance of the phenomena of consciousness that we typically think that we experience, such as free will. These conscious phenomena are in many respects what it is that must have an actual accounting, and not be merely thought of as "illusions" of consciousness. Yet the results of cognition, as we know these, must also correlate with any explanation of consciousness, so that if conscious phenomena disagree with our consciousness of cognition, it is necessary that any overall account which is made of the mind must relate the two, most likely in some causal manner. Which is to say that reason and mental perceptions are both conscious aspects that must unify, or at least be compatible, within an explanation of consciousness, neither being obviously prior to the other.

For reasons such as these there is no explanation of consciousness without the consideration of its relationship to the unconscious, for both reason and perception have unconscious roots. And especially we must understand the driving force of that area of mental processing remaining in the incomprehensible electric flashes of the unknowing, and how it affects consciousness. For consciousness arises out of the unconscious, disappearing into it again. As well, depth psychology has indicated that the subject, direction, and purpose of consciousness are profoundly affected by the forces of the deep unconscious. Consciousness is in part the tool of the unconscious, therefore, and presumably should not be treated as a phenomenon in itself, as much of the speculation about it does.

Loosely considered, then, consciousness not only has to do with ontology, but with ontogeny as well—fortunately the latter is probably more accessible, too. And there is no indication that the ontogeny of consciousness is separate from that of the unconscious, especially as it appears that consciousness develops out of its counterpart not only through development but recurrently out of unconscious sleep states, and out of anesthesia as well. It could be that consciousness is simply a special case of the unconscious, which values itself highly because it has immediate access only to that which is conscious. Admittedly, this is perhaps reason enough for such a self-valuation.

Still, not only does the stream of consciousness maintain continuity with the stream of the unconscious, it is the latter which many effectively consider to be the self. After all, it did not require depth psychology to recognize that motivation often takes place beyond consciousness. *King Lear* amply examples this in a psychological manner, while Homer located much ultimate control of humanity in the spiritual realm (which realm we subsequently locate in the unconscious). A common assumption is that "I" am whatever originates an effective mental force and achieves consciousness in some manner or another, deceitfully or not. So then one way of putting the question of consciousness is how is it that consciousness signifies the unconscious forces which energize and largely effect the objective mental realm of the conscious?

Grimm's tales cover the transitions of consciousness and of unconsciousness largely as directed by the unconscious. One of the most striking of these fables being the story of the "Frog-king", who wishes to sleep with the young princess in his bewitched frog form. Kisses may change the frog into a prince in the Disney versions, but in this tale the prince is saved by the princess giving him as hard a whack against the wall as she could, in her hate and disgust. The frog falls down from the wall as a prince, and they go to bed together after her father wills him to be her husband.

What seems obvious in the relation of this little psychic drama is the sexual force of the girl, and the violent shift of emotions and conscious content in one simultaneous transformation of the forms and forces which the sex drive energized. If anyone wishes to quibble over how representative the "Frog-king" is, thousands of more mundane, and real, narratives exist, so that this story can stand in for the others at the very least. I bring up the apparent change in the conscious content with the shift in emotion because of how plastic and phenomenal consciousness appears to be according to the shifts in the actual state of the mind—in other words, one individual can be frog or prince in the conscious mind, in spite of the fact that largely the same unconscious forces are in play in either case.

Drives and emotions perhaps should be considered to be the real mind, the forces that control the conscious and the unconscious. It is how these forces are controlled by the basic drives which yields no consensus in discussions of the mind. And this too is important to explaining consciousness. Yet this is not the subject here, as it is probably not the fundamental mystery that consciousness is. The point to be made here is the fact that the "I" today is generally no longer considered to be identical with the ego, but that the latter is frequently subject to the former, and gives us the direction in which to proceed in discussing consciousness. This model of power coming from the unconscious to the conscious has been the assumption since depth psychology, particularly Freud's, became societal context.

Perhaps one may question the role of the unconscious as the controller of our fates, but the recognition that something controls our consciousness is a very long-standing observation, accounting for gods and goddesses in the days when humanity tended toward the subjective. It gives rise to psychoanalysis in these less natural times.

Ironically, if not especially surprisingly, our alienation from nature and ourselves has given us the ability to consciously locate the unconscious control of consciousness through the evidence of correlations and experiments, even while the unconscious has apparently become less easily accessible to consciousness. This reduced accessibility seems due to the excessive overlay of perceptions— including the perceptions involving the unconscious mind. Apparently, as our consciousness drifts further from its origin it more clearly defines the major force behind it to be the unconscious mind.

And so, how something moves across the border from unconsciousness to the conscious evidently stands as an obvious scenario for how consciousness arises. A reason to think this could be the correct approach is because the change from the immediately pre-conscious to consciousness appears to not involve any drastic change in the content or configuration of the thought, picture, or whatever it happens to be, since much of it conforms with, and often informs, what was previously conscious. And it simply flows into consciousness in the case of stream-of-consciousness, at least so it seems to our consciousness, the only medium through which we are able to judge. For this reason, it may well be that consciousness is a state change. At least this is how I tend to view it.

However it is that the unconscious changes into the conscious, this surely is an essential part of the story of consciousness. Another substantial question in any probable explanation of consciousness is what happens to the makeup and structure of our cognitive content after it makes that shift into the conscious. That is, why bother with consciousness in the process of creating actions? If, as it has been said[1], consciousness is the global workspace of the mind, is it consciousness which depends on cognition's global nature, or does the universal character of thought result from consciousness? How might the two be interdependent, and to what extent?

It seems best to suppose that the unconscious has a substantial continuity with the conscious, since we experience the divide as often being not sharp, as well as because the conscious is so obviously energized by unconscious forces. Perhaps the most important factor, though, is that the ultimate purpose of the conscious mind is the same as that of the unconscious and this teleological purpose or motivation seems to be unbroken across the change from one to the other. The emotions, especially, are apparent examples of just such a continuity. In accordance with the idea that unconscious forces control the purposes both of the conscious and of the unconscious, consciousness is in fact likely to be best considered as being dominated by, and in the service of, the unconscious mind.

---

[1] Daniel Dennett particularly. *Consciousness Explained* is one of his works in which this is found.

This interpretation is likely to figure significantly in the (or at least, my) understanding of what consciousness actually is.

Having stated this much about the relation of the unconscious to consciousness, I must note too that the unconscious workings of the mind differ significantly, quite possibly crucially, with processes of consciousness. Broadly considered, one might reasonably divide the unconscious into perceptual processing along with the non-conscious rational operations of the mind on the one hand, and the emotions together with the drives on the other. And these could be roughly characterized as the externally stimulated unconscious and the internally generated unconscious, even though these can only be relative designations. For the two, as is known, do have complex interactions.

Different types of the unconscious may be as disparate as the distinction between the conscious and the unconscious. The seeming dualities of the deep ("internal") unconscious are experienced rather differently from the flux of the stream of the unconscious (which we know as it streams in to the conscious). The unconscious that most captivates the imagination, for it is at the very least a part of the imagination, is the deep unconscious, which, if it is undoubtedly partly molded by outside data and forces, nonetheless comes to a large extent from inside the mind. Still, it is the perceptions from the outside that are ultimately responsible for our response to the environment. For it is these that permit us to be nourished, also to engage in reproductive activities, and so are what evolution has fitted the nervous system to process and route. The deep unconscious can be considered to be what gives us our drives, energies, and purposes which direct us, while consciousness is involved with the entire nervous system's function of dealing with sensory output in a way that is very responsive to, and relative to, the environment.

The question of consciousness in particular, and the unconscious in general, hangs on the several means the mind uses in order to control and process the massive sensory stimulation continually driving the mental flow. One of the forces driving the whole process of coping with such a disparate input is surely our deep unconscious mental and emotional stimulation, something we apparently often sense consciously. How this would cross over from the unconscious to the conscious is a serious question, but if it can be reasonably related to the coming to consciousness of pre-conscious data (the non-deep unconscious), a major step toward understanding consciousness would be taken.

The mind is treated as a type of computer by many, and if the idea that it is much like a digital computer has now happily sunk into the past for most serious researchers and philosophers, the mind still is cast in many cases as a quantum computer or as an analog computer. Whether or not the mind really operates as a computer at all is an important question, of course, for there are crucial differences between any kind of computer and the mind. Especially important is the fact that no computer output is self-meaningful, and the mind only produces meaning via the self-meaningful. Also, a great deal of mental processing is dramatically affected by the internally produced (if externally triggered) forces mentioned above, such as the emotions.

So one may reasonably expect that the functional role of the nervous system, instead of the straight computational function, and the way in which this functional role is achieved by the various methods of processing energy and information, would be crucial to understanding the mind. And this naturally leads to proposals of causal links and the medium by which these may occur in consciousness and its correlates. This book exists as an attempt to reasonably explain the how and why of that which appears to often be so distant from reason, our ineffable experience of consciousness.

The model given here hangs substantially on this question—could processing *per se* yield consciousness, or might it lie in a different function? The answer involves the unconscious and evolutionary purposes that have formed the experience of consciousness.

Chapter 1:

Coordinating the routing of nerve impulses

The original purpose of the nerve

The original purpose of the central nervous system, which still is fundamentally important, is almost certainly the routing of the incoming action-potentials from the senses to the appropriate muscles or other tissues, in order to provide the sort of response that should be beneficial to the organism and its reproductive success. One might easily hypothesize an organism having one small sensory organ with one possible action which would commence at a certain stimulatory threshold. Then the central nervous system could easily consist of one nerve fiber connecting the single sense organ to the one responsive motor organ, the equivalent of a telegraph line exclusively connecting two buildings.

And yet this analogy between the simplest possible nervous system and the simplest possible telegraph line already breaks down at one very important difference—and in doing so illustrates a crucial dissimilarity in the way in which the organism uses its nervous system versus what happens in human-made systems. For the moment any signal can be sent down a telegraph line, complex messages can also be sent using code, since it is the case that the only entities which will care to create the telegraph can also send messages using simple on-off coding over the line. Which is to say, people can recognize meaning. On the other hand, at its most basic the transferal of an action-potential[2] between its origin in perception and its end in reaction is devoid of intermediary meanings and information processing capacities. So it is that later and more evolved capacities, the complex reactions to input that we effect, requires the development of processing and relay capabilities, and for us this development would in all likelihood have to evolve out of the same dumb nerves carrying the same dumb action-potentials as the first simple signal-carrying cells.

To make a human out of nerve firings requires a great deal of organization in order to produce the intermediaries that will route nervous activity correctly, and especially so as to allow these to route themselves according to codes and other information contained within these very action-potentials. The evolution of the human brain has yielded an astonishing system capable of dealing with extreme complexity, and apparently primarily out of the basic operation of moving action-

---

[2] To ensure understanding of terms in this book it is worth noting that an action-potential and a nerve firing are practically the same thing—and the two are used interchangeably in this book.

potentials from their origins to the place where reactions to stimuli will produce the preferred responses. Certainly it is the means and intricacy of the complex routing of action-potentials that makes all of the difference between our nervous system and the primitive type.

The focus of most brain research and ideas about cognition and consciousness is typically on this complex mediation, and on the structures of the brain that is our primary intermediate. Perhaps this is as it should be, yet on the other hand it does obscure the essential function and character of the nervous system, since it implies that the proper function of the brain—of the mind—is accurate information processing and as exact a modeling of the world as is practically possible. While these may be supplemental and accessory functions in some cases, the essential purpose of the mind appears to be no different than that of a reflex—the propagation of action-potentials to produce a successful response to a set of sensory-derived action-potentials. To do so well happens to require a good deal of information processing, but at the core of brain function remains the fundamental purpose of routing (and maintaining) activation energy.

If the foregoing picture is taken as a reasonable starting point, which at least this book does, the sorts of methods of moving activation energies needs also to be considered. For indeed digital computers are given nearly the same task as the nervous system, that of taking in data in the form of energy and in turn producing a response consisting of an energy output heavy in information. The difference is that the digital computer can only route information by processing it logically (aside from the information in the wiring, etc.). So in the computer, the direction and routing of signals necessarily depends on data being defined according to logic.

This cannot be what happens in the simplest possible nervous systems, where nothing is known, equated, or logically produced (in the sense of a previously known logic). It is necessary to investigate into what sorts of logic, what mechanisms for routing, arise in the nervous system for insuring that the output of action-potentials produce an evolutionarily advantageous reaction in responding to a certain input of action-potentials.

Two ways of shaping output

Two basic forms of producing output seem to exist. These are the reflex action broadly considered, and the rational processes, the latter often explained through neural nets. In the regard to the former, however much processing of signals may occur within the reflex, it is nevertheless primarily a matter of linking up nervous input through the various pathways and synapses to produce a desirable nervous output. No actual "solution" to the input is produced by whatever processing of information occurs apart from routing to the output, nor is there any "proposal" of an appropriate answer, or "correct" reaction to the information contained in the incoming action-potentials. For the pathway of nerves simply means that one production follows another, and the input is in a way merely equal to, or causal of, the output.

A complicating factor arises even in such simple systems as, for instance, the patellar reflex, the normal response to being hit just below the kneecap. And it is that outgoing nervous impulses must occur at the correct frequency and be kept coordinated proportional to output geometries. Input from beyond the just the triggered sensors, ergo learning (with some genetic and developmental components), must happen at even this level of signal processing. Yet it presumably is fair to observe that this is still essentially a routing function, albeit complex, with coordination and frequency modulation of output being produced in a largely predetermined reaction.

This is all very well recognized, furthermore, reflexivity, habit, and the various forms of reaction affecting human behavior and thought is to varying degrees noted (also sometimes condemned), among those who study mind and brain. In making judgments about such modes of human behavior, higher mental functions must be invoked, for even those intellectuals who deny the meaning of higher functions would not be able to do so had they not at least once considered certain modes of thought, typically including reason, to be more valuable than others. That is to say, the "higher mental functions" may indeed not be intrinsically more valuable, rather the human tendency is to value these more, and thus to lend an authority and priority to those who would deny the authority and priority of "higher functions". However that may be, appealing to this prejudice may be the only way to allow its negation an equal footing, and thus equal consideration, with its affirmation. This is the conceit of deconstructionism, but perhaps it could have a role in the (rare) right hands.

Reason's detractors therefore example the appeal to the rational

And thus it is that reason and computation are valued by humans. Once the "spiritual realm", a difficult to categorize "higher function", competed with knowledge and intelligence in value, but fairy tales, myths, and legends have long ceased to really be produced, replaced by rumor, the category to which "urban myths" truly belong. Spirituality is worthy of both non-reductive consideration, which cannot be done in a book (even a book of poetry really only demonstrates it), and of reductive consideration. However, at this point that clear alternative to simple reflex in the production of output—rational processing—requires a short consideration of its extent.

In doing so, it should be noted that there is not possible, naturally, any clear and certain quantification of the degree to which our mental activity consists of rational processing. Even so it must be considerable, for we have capacities far beyond any demonstrated in other animals. Some of this is cultural, yet given that, *Homo sapiens* as a speaking creature inevitably creates an objectivizing, rational (at least in part) culture.

If one demurs that Jung and others make a good case for subjective "primitive" societies, dream-times in aboriginal cultures, this is all very well. But if one attends to the narratives and myths of these peoples, to the rational spatial and temporal context, as well as to the ordering of the magical and the subjective content, one can see that even our subjective world is rendered into a rational order for the purpose of "intersubjectivity". For instance, simple numbers, such as the number three, dominate the order of at least Grimm's stories. But this sort of observation is not made to disparage (much) the ideas of intersubjectivity, rather it is to make the notice that the semantics of intersubjectivity also requires an order which is rationally (which is not the same as "consciously") determined.

The foregoing is written in order to give due credit to our rational capacities, partly because this book is mostly about important non-rational processes, and I do not wish to short-change logic *as such*. But it is also to serve the argument that most rationality tends to be structural, as well as part of the internally coordinating mental processes. In fact, all rationality probably exists ultimately for the coordination of input and output in the nervous system, and so is not necessarily the truth of the world. To contend for this by the examples both of logic and of mathematics appears easy enough, simply by considering why most calculations, and rational constructions, are performed at all. For logic merely deals with the correlation of what is, and not the "thing itself". The logical and the rational are clearly highly valued human capacities—however these are valued within the process of obtaining results. Pragmatically this means routing—and relating—input potentials into an appropriate output.[3]

The rational probably comes from, and evolves for the sake of, routing nervous content

Tentatively, then, logic and rationality may be thought of as first appearing out of the ordering of action-potentials, in both the spatial and temporal dimensions. I do believe that rationality is ultimately subservient to the nervous system's presumed original function, that of merely routing action-potentials from the sensory to the motor areas. Nevertheless, it need not be so in order to consider the essentiality of rationality in both the "reflex actions", and in the normal switching and triggering functions of the brain. While recognizing the

---

[3] Of course there are issues of magnitude and quality in this process, but this is a broad consideration that should be considered to include these aspects in the routing, as indeed these two along with others would affect even the single neuron as it is extended between sensor and motor.

value of the rational in consciousness, we must first consider how this operates within presumed non-conscious nervous systems.

Space, time—and logic—in routing

Two modes of the mediation of the firings of nerves presumably characterize the more primitive and less conscious actions of the nervous system (and, I argue, these are ultimately responsible for the higher and conscious processes as well). These correspond to the spatial and temporal aspects inherent in our world, which, as in other systems, are crucial factors in the simplest and the most complex of routing schemes between the sensory and the motor functions. One may of course think of spatiality and temporality either separately or according to their interactions with each other.

The most fundamental spatial effects in routing are, unsurprisingly, fairly obvious. In our hypothesized most basic nervous system consisting of one nerve, the action-potential from the sensory area must end up in the appropriate motor tissue. One way this could be configured is that a worm's tail has a touch sensor that is directly connected to a muscle of the worm that causes the worm's body to bend in an escape or attack mode, perhaps in an action that could be both or either. In a more evolved system the ability to "choose" several routes for the various action-potentials to take allows a rather greater flexibility in the response, not to mention a considerable rise in complexity.

Even in nervous systems capable of switching, a number of spatial aspects of routing remain obvious enough. It appears, though, that only in the simplest of systems is the timing aspect relatively simple conceptually. Timing at its simplest results from whatever the single nerve provides as the condition for the velocity of the action-potential. However, when multiple "nerves" exist, what seems to be the most interesting aspect of ordering is not the spatial dimension of signaling, but the temporal. For while single pathway action-potentials could surely be useful, once more than one "nerve" exists, coordination of "nerves" in time becomes essential to produce significantly more useful results across the space of multiple "nerves".[4] Especially since action-potentials are produced probabilistically by synapses, a very important aspect of nervous systems in general is in all probability simply the coordination of nerve signals, thereby canceling out the randomness of their propagation.

---

[4] Note that the conductor of an action-potential need hardly be a nerve *per se* (hence "nerve" is here put in quotes), for cells typically spread charges across their outer membranes, and many allow inter-cellular conductance as well, most notably (aside from nerves) muscle cells. I use "nerve" for whatever conducts an action-potential not primarily to coordinate and continue an action (as in muscles), but principally to convey an impulse to act

Relations of nerve signals producing "rationalized" sets of signals

To be sure, this coordination has more than one source, in some cases likely including the logical operations, along with various forms of intersection and combining of signals. But there are probably two coordinating forces that would be the most primitive, and I believe these probably remain the most important. The first source of coordinating force would seem to be signals that are somehow dominant (probably in energy) and that in varying ways force a certain conformity onto weaker signals, perhaps by dominating the stimulation of synapses. The second and related force of coordination would be the tendency of oscillations, waves, and any other periodic forms of energy to synchronize if a sufficient means for energy transferal exists.[5] It is this latter phenomenon, when understood as occurring through induction (arguing for this mechanism being the primary purpose of this book), which not only allows for the relation of information across the various action-potentials, but it is also one that quite possibly affords the *earliest* form of information processing in the nervous system.

A fact learned relatively early in most physics courses is that pendulums hanging from a single beam, as, for instance, swings on a swing set, rather quickly begin to swing in unison, or in some other sort of synchronicity. Electrical impulses in close enough proximity tend to react similarly, thanks to the ability of energy to transfer via magnetic fields and the resultant inductional process. The electro-chemical impulses in the action-potentials similarly synchronize, apparently, an essential feature in uniform, patterned, and sequential phenomena. It should be noted that in the process must occur the transferal of information-laden energy potentials as causal force, seemingly transferred by means of a process of induction that would be much like electrical induction.

At this juncture it is the function as well as the quasi-logic resulting from the finely divided field of nervous energy that are worth noting in such a synchronization. Without order and logic, both in the arrangement of the nerves and in the arrangements and temporal relations of nervous impulses, there could be no meaningful ("meaningful" probably at this level meaning coordinated and associated) transfer of information within the system of nerves. The meaning (or "meaning") that would exist in a single nerve would be lost were it not ordered in relation to that in other nerves. The caveat to be made here is that this still leaves the *whole* without any certain meaning. However, it must be the case that accurate apprehension of even the "non-rational" (for example qualia or arbitrary

---

[5] See, for example, Gray, C.M., Konig, P., Engel, A.K., and Singer, W. (1989). "Synchronization of oscillatory responses in visual cortex: a plausible mechanism for scene segmentation". Proceedings of the Conference on Synergetics of the Brain.

shapes) is highly dependent on the underlying logic of the nervous system. And anyway, lack of meaning in the whole is our experience, which evidently drives us to seek further knowledge for the sake of context.

The previously mentioned spatial ordering (partly, surely not entirely, due to genetics) does, of course, fulfill part of the logical arrangement of nervous impulses, but the synchronizing activity of the nervous system provides another portion of this ordering. It is worth noting at this point that a truly centralized nervous system is probably not necessary for such an ordering of activities when provoked by the action-potentials resulting from fairly simple sensory patterns. The combination of spatial ordering and impulse coordination from sensory input to motor output may very well allow for appropriate simple responses such as a *Hydra* (a flatworm) moving in accordance with its environment.

Unique information would also shape the nerve signals

Apart from the spatial ordering of nerves, the various ways of synchronization and the establishment of other rhythms and harmonies is probably one of the primary methods of coordinating actions. Yet it need not be the only way of non-spatially creating the forms of movements and reactions, for inductions across the nerves must be very complex and rich in unique data. Even if it were given that there is a point at which synchronization reaches a threshold for the production of activity (not really assumed in this book, but a possibility), the inevitable divergence of action-potentials from this synchronicity means that a complex set of interactions must be superimposed on the underlying order, and even that order would have a unique shape in the brain. In any event, all of these interactions, whether synchronizing and harmonizing, or contrarily refusing to do so, would crucially involve timing.

Since the geometry of the nerves is fairly stable per given set of action-potentials, whether these are coordinated or non-coordinated action-potentials, timing is what can make the difference between the various sensations and the various resulting actions. Both of these types of differentiated sets of action-potentials are information-rich, unconscious during much of their existence, and it seems nearly inevitable that they would hold much of their data among, rather than within, the action-potentials.

Some nerve signals are no doubt coded, in a manner of speaking, while the others have a certain temporal and spatial arrangements that might or might not also be considered coding. What is necessary, then, is to consider how a "code" might be handled by evolved creatures that by no means are born with *a priori* knowledge of the world.

Chapter 2:

Information is an unavoidable issue in routing and switching

Codes and symbols

The simplest symbol is merely an action. Movements, words thought, words spoken, words received, all could be thought of as being about equally symbol, equally action, with no necessary categorical psychological differences between word and action.[6] Importantly, codes as we normally define them depend on symbols of various sorts as the basic units for these codes. Symbols, actions, words, none of these should be seen mainly as codes, rather, as effects of the sensations which give rise to them, be the sensations internal or external.

Consider that red is signified by a certain sequence of firings in certain nerves, just as different arrangements signify other colors.[7] This sequence is often termed a code. But is it? What or who could ever decode a cipher like this one? Definitely there is a code-like aspect to such a sequence, and given a certain perspective, there is no problem with considering it to be a code—a researcher, for one, might treat it as code. However, in the more usual meaning, "code" implies the concealment of a recognizable meaning under unrecognizable symbolization, the transferal of meaning through arbitrary yet consistent designations that substitute for the symbolization of that meaning. The trouble with the matter of nerve coding is that the quale "red" lacks a meaning of this sort. Colors have no more intrinsic meaning than do the nerve impulses that give rise to the phenomena of colors, so what relationship could "nerve codes" have to colors?

There is no meaning, or sense in its very self, for which to "code"

The whole question of qualia is vexed, of course, and colors are not really translatable, although symbols can be designated for them. However, this is true of all sensory experience, and of the way in which we synthesize objects and their parts out of qualia. The problem is that the nervous system generally lacks

---

[6] While it is true that actions and words are not strictly exchangeable in all cases, words fail to substitute for actions in much the way that, for instance, hysterical actions fail to substitute for verbalization. So it is difficult to give priority of one over the other. Furthermore, freedom to act (for example, in revenge) might be able to substitute for words while hysterical actions do not.

[7] The issue of color coding is certainly more complex than given here, but the text is close enough to the truth for what is being exemplified.

meaningful points of basic reference (except as we create "meaning"), and indeed the common belief that meaning is simply conferred in its original instance appears to be unavoidable (if exceedingly complex). If one considers the nervous system to have primarily the same function as the hypothesized first nerves, that is, to transfer action-potentials from their points of origin to remote locations, one may understand why. For the sequence of action-potentials signifying red is simply an effecter of subsequent actions, and presumably it produces the sensation of red only as a part of the causal chain (or possibly as a side effect or epiphenomenon) on the way to the desired effect.

Hence the "meaning" of the set of nerve signals, or rather, its lack of meaning, carries over to our sensation of the quale "red". There appears to be a correlation between the definite, but meaningless in essence, "code" for red, and the lack of meaning in the percept existing as that color[8]. To sense red is not necessarily the same as unloading any meaning or emotion, although its further effect, either through the perception of qualia or otherwise, may evoke either. Or, it may more directly become a part of the nervous potentiation for action if it is so routed, as seems to be the best interpretation for the quick perceptions and actions of the athlete. The quale's effects are not unlike those of its presumptive nervous correlate (including, so far as we can tell, the emotional effect) when existing apart from the perception and consciousness of the quale, that is, when the athlete acts according to color without consciousness of it *per se* or when color subconsciously sets a mood. So there is little reason to think that a quale is effectively anything but a potential for action, and it seems best to characterize it according to the evidence that it is such a potential rather than according to phenomenal and speculative ideas.

Qualia, then, evidently are somehow the results of sets of action-potentials, and apparently they do not change in their manner of effect simply by becoming conscious percepts (although they are probably more general when they are conscious qualia). Meaningless on their own, qualia, and all sense-data, matter in regard to the effects these produce. And because the central nervous system relates a large portion of incoming sensory action-potentials with at least some of the rest of the sense data, what matters is the nature of their relations in such a context. It should as well be noted here that these contextual relationships are why we tend to be able to pick out objects from the environment—because the closer relationships of information start to be habitually related and contextualized after a period of learning.

---

[8] This is not to ignore the fact that red has meaningful and emotional relations. It seems to have emotional overtones different from those of blue, yet the sensation need not evoke meaning or emotion, at least not noticeably. My own position is tentatively that the sensation, the quale, is therefore prior to its "evocations" of meaning and emotion.

Types of interactions of nerves

Now to return to the interactions of action-potentials. So far I have barely mentioned one of the most important parts of the nervous system, the synapses. This is because these are more like a part of the structure of the nerves, could be considered as a part of them, and are relatively stable over the short run while changeable over a longer period of time. Synapses and the arrangement of nerves may very well be considered to be the "hard-wiring" of the brain, if one is considering the brain as similar to an "analog computer" (true in only some aspects), instead of a digital computer. It is my belief that the brain is ultimately only concerned to route action-potentials in the optimal manner, and any actual "computing" is due to the subsystems which facilitate this activity. Nevertheless, the routing or "hard-wiring" also requires a sort of "instruction set" or programming to direct the forms and activities of a wired-up nervous system.

Whatever the information handling capacities inherited and developed in the nerve arrangements and synapses, nothing can prepare the mind for the ever-new contingencies of the world. Unlike computers, the brain deals with the unknown, and this it does because it can continually route and re-route action-potentials according to information that it picks up. Indeed, it is precisely because the brain is mostly without specific reference points and meanings that it is capable of dealing with the surprisingly alien world from which it arose, for it manages to assimilate information from that world. We can cope with cobras by ascribing to them magical powers, or synaptic poisons, and both descriptions are at least partly adequate for action. Mass, too, is something we can symbolize with our massless concepts, so it can be considered either a primordial substance, or a form of energy involved with quarks, among other possibilities.

The point being that we can cope with the information in our sets of action-potentials by symbolizing it as either magical or rational systems (or in other ways), both of which, however, depend on the stability of some of the more fundamental elements of action-potentials. Ultimately, of course, much depends on the stability of the nerve correlates of qualia.

But it is crucial that the only of new information for the instructions used in dealing with contingencies is from the same source as the contingencies, that being the mass of perception-derived action-potentials interacting with data in the nervous system, primarily the central nervous system. Were not a great many of the usual sorts of action-potentials more or less routinely routed, joined, divided, or whatever switching is demanded[9] (along with data transfer occurring in

---

[9] That is to say, most of the nerve impulses are "known", from memory, from deep drives and archetypes etc., or from nerve shapes, and both the original and conditioned synaptic responses.

inductive arrays), and the new nerve impulses correlated to time and space along with the rest, the action resulting from the nerve signals would be random. Yet the critical step is that new and essentially "meaningless" information enters the unconscious and conscious nervous streams, and subsequently forms a response, often appropriate, although inappropriate responses are not rare. Fortunately feedback tends to allow refinement in the cases of inappropriate responses where the organism survives.

Harmonic interactions

These novel responses, especially the less deliberated types, will often be felt to be magical, having little or no obvious basis for actually being correct. Historically, the Pythagoreans understood harmonies in this way, for the mathematics involved had no visible foundation in experience, yet this knowledge yielded apparently significant and usable results. To be sure, in this case there is some empirical knowledge involved, but the sensation of dealing rationally with unknown principles and causes can be similar in this case with the realization that one has, for example, achieved the power of gunpowder through the mystery (prior to chemistry) of the substances involved. Or perhaps that one has found the way to charm the opposite sex despite its unknowns and unknowables.

The problem of novel information

Thinking is hard work. It is easy to see why in such instances, since these involve formulating responses to the unknown, although not to the entirely unknown. Of course it is useless to think in a number of cases, though I add quickly that it is in general not an accidental or superfluous activity. It is probably not inappropriate to observe that calculation and deliberation, that is, the involvement of the brain's computing and logical abilities, is not primary. For as we know, creativity is the spontaneous production of a response, while rationality and deliberation are the development and judgment of this creativity. Both modes of thought are essential, since creativity has little value without learning and judgment, while the latter exist to evaluate the flash of creative magic, that quirky Gestaltic interaction of action-potentials which suddenly sees the proper response emerge out of seemingly random interactions. Clearly a great deal of thought and deliberation is more than just numinous objects arising magically from the interactions of nervous impulses. Yet I maintain that it is this fluorescent glow of creation which is prior to and more important than the deadly sameness of the computations of the hypothesized neural nets. Creative interactions of nerves are what provide the substance upon which judgment and calculation can act.

One evidence for the relatively uncalculated nature of our responses to novelty is that the speed with which much of it occurs is simply too great. Particularly when an immediate response is necessary, the result is too quick for any significant processing by the rather slow action-potentials and synapse activity in the brain. Although *recognition* is common in such instances, it must be that data in the novel perception—without much computational processing—must be a part of the "instruction set" which guides the rest of the "wiring" and "switching" which also make up a part of the novel response. What other information is there for the purpose?

For we must recognize that there are no predetermined instructions for the *new* information in the novel percept, even though parameters exist for it. The pre-existing means of processing available to such novelty is whatever occurs within the habitual response, that is, little, other than phase changes, diffusion, and whatever syntheses and mixing naturally takes place in the shift from sensing to action. The new data cannot possibly provoke an immediate response except through its causal effect of informed energetic force, for the novel information is simply "in the mix", molding the action, and being molded by the same action.

On the other hand, there is the tendency we have to make an analogical "judgment"[10] of "equality" that occurs in the case of recognition, or less nobly, the imposition of prior knowledge or prejudice upon perceptions. This is Nietzsche's complaint about logic and rationality, that these are impositions.[11] Such projection is well known, thanks to experience, Nietzsche, and other thinkers, and to some degree it does lessen the impact that novel information has. Nevertheless, there are numerous instances when no analog can really be taken as equivalent to past experience. Instead we frequently are forced to construct new actions almost immediately in times of crisis, or conversely, over time and through very complex interactions if we have the leisure to reflect on the new knowledge.

Important to mention at this juncture is that even when projection forces data into habits, types, and stereotypes (notably, often directly into perceptions), it happens as our ability to impose order on the uncertainty of novel responses. To be sure, there is resistance to acting in novel and dangerous situations if these are avoidable. In spite of the resistance, when novelty is inescapable the new data often shape the response to a fair degree, or how else could it be a response to the actual situation?

---

[10] There is a good deal of confusion about what constitutes judgment versus "simple recognition" and the like, and philosophers like Husserl have waxed boring on it. Probably judgment and recognition are merely locations on a continuum—and at least that is the assumption used in this book.

[11] An instance of Nietzsche's treatment of logic is in *The Gay Science*, section 111.

Considerations of projected information

The power of projecting rationality and analogous identifications onto less certain sensory information suggests that, as much as data dominate and control eventual output, it is in truth the potential for action (as in, "action-potential") of nervous impulses that is the crucial driving force of the human central nervous system. That is to say, the "drive to rationalize" our viewpoint has a decided effect in our actions, expectedly coming via the power of action-potentials affecting the shape of perceptual nerve firings within their context. The foregoing is stated here mainly as a caveat (though partly to foreshadow the later discussion), since this fact could be forgotten in discussions of the crucial interactions of information in the nervous system.

Then, it may be seen that human computation and rationality could readily add an extra dimension onto the more primitive function of simply moving (and maintaining, etc.) the force necessary to trigger action from the sensory organs to the motor organs. Our rational computing power grants us a greater ability to form the response, by being able to enhance within one's field of perception the rational forms in the field. Also what has been learned (such as an animal's vulnerabilities) from experience could in the same manner re-enforce portions of the totality of sensations.

Humans do have rational capabilities which are no doubt developed through experience, but which surely receive some of their potential from genetic factors. On the other hand, the process of recognizing non-geometric shapes, and non-rational forms, also relies upon the above mentioned sensory component which is available from the memory. This is to note here the well-known fact that much is merely remembered and associated. And this information, like any new data at a given time, had to once exist contextually across sets of action-potentials. Emotions, drives, and possibly something akin to Jungian archetypes also have impacts on such information. The sensory component, though, existing in our partly rational or rationalized nervous system, does apparently provide the most data in the collections of information that inform our responses.

Information apparently shapes action during routing and switching

The interesting part of the shaping of, and of the impositions on, the sensory field is that it looks similar to the honing and shaping of the actions that we learn as a repertoire. Probably there is no great divide between what happens in perception and what occurs in performing actions, with the primary difference being that perceptual information may shape an action which we are able to decide against doing.

What is more, the perception and action even seem commonly to occur during one action, like when a baseball player swings his bat at a ball while being intensely aware of the motions of the ball, and less so the bat. The action and the sensing would seem then to be similarly effective to the action. The dependence of the relationship is evidently on the sensory data—and it is the more conscious of the two. In experiences like those of the batter, we concentrate on perception in order to hone action, which appears oddly similar to the direct sensory throughput of the single nerve as hypothesized earlier in this book.

It could be argued, against the fairly direct throughput I having been arguing as the most likely for much of experience, that indeed responses are modified and shaped, rather than simply transmitted. The question is, how can it be shaped by switching and routing through synapses and nerves? To be sure, I have been making the case for information itself as being the most flexible and fluid "programming" data. But all the same this information could not so act if there were not a great deal of stability in the "hard-wiring" that allows the relation of these data, via switching and the combination and divergence of nervous impulses, among other functions. The problem being, of course, that the "hardwiring" would seem not likely to produce and hone novel results from new information, instead becoming confused and garbled due to mismatch that would only become worse through successive synapses. Synapses have the on-off response that digital computers have, after all, and despite the differences, novel information would quickly be reduced to the same thing as different magnitudes of conventional information.

The comparison with computers that may be made is that different results indeed do depend on the invariant procedures of rational computing. Different data treated the same way, become in this manner, differentiated or combined. However, the contrast between brain and computer comes most prominently into view when we consider that information in the brain generally lacks pre-given references, at least in many of the aspects of the information. Also, not only new information shows up, new conjunctions and interactions of even conventional information are presumably not rare, but frequent (though generally through changes produced by new knowledge). The data with which the brain deals is in continual flux even while an apparent stability of qualia, triggers, habits, and reactions maintains a necessary coherence within the whole.

Data shift the contexts of information in the brain

It is not easy to explain the differences between brain and computer, especially since both have stable features, and still the brain manages to treat information far more fluidly. However I believe that the brain's departure from the computer's rigidity coincides with the point at which the information in the brain partially decouples from action-potentials. This can happen physically, as will be considered later, or simply contextually—which happens to explain at least some of the brain's fluidity.

Nervous impulses are laden with information, of course. Typically this information is considered as the account of the brain's non-static data. Perhaps this is so, but the way the human nervous system works is that it produces the reactions of the organism. And it is for this reason that, when it happens, the relatively direct throughput of data into action in the nervous system (along with input from memory, with other sources) implies that synapses and nerves cooperate for the sake of synchronization and coordination of output into the proper efferent nerves. It is this that is the "purpose" (or anyway, one purpose) of the brain, rather than the reproduction of reality from the image of an object or set of objects.

There are two reasons to be considered here in regard to why it is that information becomes an issue in a system that is actually geared to routing action-potentials. One obvious reason is that some information processing helps to figure out where nerve signals should go. However, this processing capability must have been a later evolutionary development than the other reason—which, in fact, must have arisen as a reaction to the following problem. During evolution one of the earlier issues involving information must have been the fact that data contained in sensory input are not the same as data contained in the output.

In the very simplest organisms the "input" data must surely have been virtually the same as the "output" data. Further along in evolution, even while sequence of action-potentials might have continued to remain largely the same between input and output (or not), the differences in the incoming data would have to be coordinated into the output, for instance, into changing the direction of the organism's flight from danger. In this way, increasingly the information in the nerve signals would itself necessarily direct the outgoing impulses. The more decoupled action-potentials became from a specific output (as response became more variable, that is), the more the information within the totality of nerve impulses must have guided the actual flow of action-potentials. Which is to say that data would become contextualized.

Looking ahead to where this scenario is going, it seems that it is precisely the data that at least partially decouple from the mere flow of impulses in nerves that are what become conscious. And it is this information, no longer merely a part of the nerve signal, that is capable of acting as "software", thus able to direct the remaining parts of the flow shaping it into an appropriate output. This is the case that remains to be made.

Chapter 3:

The difference between information and action-potentials

Information is in the differences between nervous signals

Much more information can probably exist in the differences between nerve signals than in the signals themselves. And not all subscribe to the viewpoint that the brain's dynamic, active information is merely the sum of the information in each and every action-potential. Nevertheless, the default position is typically that information is "coded", and that one coded symbol means one thing—a quasi-digital, or Morse-code like, view of the brain's working information.

It is natural for people to think so, for it would seem that the information in the differences between nerve impulses would have to be processed by some sort of computer, and for many the only computer available biologically is the collection of neurons in the brain. By analogy, computers are presently used often to extract information from differential outputs—but not from themselves. Neural nets and the like have been proposed to provide the structures for computation within the brain. However, the original and the typical operations of the brain (such as associations) could hardly depend on such specialized and relatively slow functions, nor could a substantially digital operation deal with novel situations—and it is the novel situations that substantially make the brain, ordering its development by forming outputs in new ways. What is interesting by comparison of the brain with computers is that this comparison would imply that information is at the very least available to be extracted from complexes of nervous impulses and their differentials, that the brain would not necessarily be limited to the data which are embodied merely within the sum of its action-potentials.

The surprise would be if evolution of the brain did not find a way to exploit a good portion of its available information, including differential information. In the usual depiction of brain operation, such an assumption would not appear to be supported, since in fact it would there appear that much of what happens is simply the routing of input impulses into motor output of one type or another, as has previously been noted. However, to continue re-stating the case made before, while neural net "computation" and various inputs of information affect and partly effect the response, it is the information within the complex input that is surely the most crucial factor in directing and switching the routes of the appropriate efferent action-potentials.

Typically there is a complex output, and it is the information within input, plus what has been evoked, that really constitutes enough data to route action-potentials into a useful response. It could even be that the data (in original form) necessarily disappear into the response in order to fully inform the ensuing action. The point being that in the flexible and relatively fluid system that the brain is, information must have a decisive influence on routing, rather than the latter being determined simply by the circuitry of neurons. Otherwise, how would circuits be able to change usefully?

That seems obvious enough once it is stated. The usual way, though, of viewing brain activity is that it is predominately, if not exclusively, due to codes, computations, and "decisions" in the complex of nerves that is the brain. The brain's complexity, since it is not understood at all well, becomes the miracle that happens, a modern day substitute for the soul or spirit. Somewhere in there the decision is made, somehow consciousness is produced. Consciousness especially is indeed considered to be a mystery, while the "decision" is typically accepted as, to be sure, incompletely comprehended, yet is nonetheless presumed to be relatively straightforward and explainable in the broader sense.

Problems with the probabilistic reactions of nerves and synapses

This belief in the comprehensibility of the "decision" is due to the fact that, for the most part, nerves and synapses work in a fairly straightforward fashion to initiate and propagate nervous signals. Even though nerves lack the precision and one-to-one correspondence of electronic circuitry, it might seem that a probabilistic, analog sort of computation along with on-off synaptic output could account for brain activity even so. What apparently is forgotten in this scenario is that the loss of data would quickly become severe if probabilistic propagation and processing predominated in the brain. For the contextual and complexed information would quickly be lost as cumulative losses destroyed the knowledge that depends for its usability on non-probabilistic temporal and spatial relationships. This problem may not be as severe in the more specific (pre-conscious) processing centers, but when the data are more global, probabilistic propagation will destroy and scatter contextual knowledge. Inevitably, some information must undoubtedly be destroyed, as we could never use the totality of the data input, yet we obviously are able to preserve and use a great deal of our sensory intake.

The problem of the seemingly unaccountable ability of the brain to process information beyond its slow nerve speed is, I believe, related to the brain's capacity for being able to correlate, and to keep from confusing, very complex data. Of course, these two difficult to explain brain abilities would indeed be addressed in computers by similar and overlapping solutions. But in the brain it is the correlations of data, not just architecture and quantitative informational interactions as in computers, that have to coordinate and produce the "coded" nervous outputs from out of the "coded" nervous inputs. No exact timer or strictly referenced cause and effect across the actions of nerves and synapses is available to the brain to keep track of information in an ordered manner, as one would find in the digital computer.

The caveat that should be repeated here is that it should not be thought that this is necessarily the case in all of the non-cognitive, non-conscious portions of the brain. Presumably the large visual cortex indeed manages, with codes, perhaps some reference timing, and maybe by keeping track of nerve firings that come in at the same time, to process signals in a relatively deterministic fashion. This seems necessary for our ability to use sight to reference ourselves to the world—that is, to keep the reference frame stable. The problem with deterministic processing arises where information must reliably transfer flexibly into one or several of a number of possible outcomes, sometimes including outcomes which were never before attempted. How do our brains manage and order the fluidity of the mind that is possible when it is working at its best?

The question of the high-speed combinations of information in the moving animal

The binding problem is frequently cited as one of the greatest difficulties in thinking about consciousness[12]. Fortunately, any possible solution to it is very nearly the possible solution of how the mind can be flexible without information becoming de-correlated—or essentially random—within the brain. It seems that we must conclude that information simply cannot remain localized within the action-potentials of nerves. Otherwise the only real question of brain would be the relatively simple matter of how nerve signals arise at synapses, propagate, then terminate again at other synapses (or simply transfer through electrical synapses). Anyone who is impressed with the precision movements of athletes, or perhaps, gibbons and cats, could understand that another considerable "binding problem" is how information precisely (and very quickly) transfers across the nervous signals to be able to adjust the shape of the sets of outgoing action-potentials. After all, these are probably significantly unlike the correlations of the sets of incoming nerve signals.

It is well known that the various nerve impulses do in fact affect each other directly through synapses for the purpose of coordinating and shaping the totality of impulses in a set of action-potentials. One must ask, however, if this process could explain the coordination of information in the areas of the brain that process information generally? It has already been argued that probabilistic systems of nerves could not track data well enough in the more universal system of data processing functioning in cognition as known via consciousness. Even

---

[12] Essentially the "binding problem" is the question of how information presumably carried in "separate" nervous impulses can join into a largely unitary consciousness.

so, the case can be made that the problem is especially acute in the process of the combination of information.

Trouble arises in the standard model of information processing in which dendrites feed data into synapses—although this undoubtedly is one way the brain deals with information. In this model, the quantitative force in the combination of nerve impulses is thought to decide the probability of the synapse propagating an action-potential downstream[13]. This is a useful method for routing and quantifying the appropriate action-potentials for the creation of the appropriate efferent action-potentials.[14] It is not, however, the sort of thing that can preserve information except in a degraded form. In such summary and quantitative reactions, the data feeding into the synapse are destroyed as such, losing form, timing, and context. The routing of action-potential can be successful in this type of process, but even though that is ultimately the goal of the nervous system, for the sake of precise transmission of knowledge and action the data must be processed and related at least partially before disappearing into quantitative summations in the synapses. In fact the two effects, information processing, then the routing of action-potentials, could well be conceived of as two different processes. The two are not, of course, entirely separate, nevertheless I maintain that they are also not entirely the same, especially not in regard to information interactions.

Combining separate categories of information from different senses

Not a lot is known about how inputs into nerve cells combine into axonal output, let alone when the process is repeated through several nerves. But it seems likely that an efferent motor action-potential may be, and probably typically is, the result at some remove of inputs from several senses. If for simplicity's sake we were to consider an instance of sensory inputs coming from two senses, the loss of data from the original information content as it arose through cognition should be able to exemplify the problems inherent in the combination of most sorts of categorically different information.

So suppose there are two nerve impulses (representing two sets of these impulses) coming from dendrites and combining to produce one synaptic firing (standing for one set of these firings) and thus one motor nerve signal. Maybe the input impulses are the codings for a certain audio tone, and those for green, and the synapse is sensitive to both signals. Then the synapse either sets off a

---

[13] Of course the story is rather more complex than this, with some synapses changing their responses to stimulation over time— "learning", that is.

[14] Probably some sort of version of this is used in the case of rationalizations and logical judgments. Yet it is no doubt more than that. The production of appropriately sized motor impulses for the particular nerve and downstream synapses being a likely function.

nerve firing or it does not, based on the information in these two very different sources and how the synapse responds to such data. What then does the outgoing nerve firing mean?

Could a specific synapse, which responded only to that tone and that color preserve the incoming information in the action-potential produced? Perhaps some such synapses exist, but far too many combinations of data are possible for that to be a general solution. So even if there may be synapses that are as specific as that, it is impossible that they are responsible for processing in the more general sections of the brain where information is necessarily combined in a presumably much more flexible manner than such hypothetical synapses. It is essential to notice that the sorts of combinations that are necessarily made of disparate data cannot be made with such specified responses.

Or, possibly more importantly, quite different sets of incoming action-potentials can yield similar, if somewhat differing, sets of outgoing action-potentials (the same as saying that different sensing situations can produce similar motor actions). The specific information in the action-potentials that trigger certain actions therefore becomes entirely lost in the combinations that eventually yield the appropriate actions. This is an essential result of the need to produce the proper response to our environment, yet such essentially crude and data-destroying combinations of information are inadequate for relating and processing data.

It is thus easy to see how truly meaningless the combination of two sets of data from different senses really is, yet how necessary this sort of reduction must be in some cases. In fact, however, combining lines, points, and reducing, for example, the richness of the visual field to the patterns of the Gestalts, is similarly destructive of data, as well as being essential to our limited range of responses. What is troubling in such a model of the brain as consisting of nerves plus synapses and primarily processing data via summation gates is that the causal force of information differentials is so thoroughly lost in these combinations effected via quantitative summation. This is true even if we grant that a number of filters (synapses, I believe) must exist to produce precisely such an effect in the case of some, but crucially *not* other, data.

Rationality is almost certain to depend in part on summary judgments such as result from multiple dendrite feeds into single synapses. The problem is that, as numerous critics such as Nietzsche have complained, rationality is primarily an imposition on the data within the mind, and thus on the evidence of the senses. Yet rationality does seem to correspond with the world (ignoring the huge problem of evidence for this, and instead simply accepting our practical, pragmatic experiences for the present discussion). We know this because there are many instances where we can distinguish rational projections on sensory data from sensory phenomena themselves, and we know that frequently the two fairly dovetail. So it is probably safe to assume that summary actions produced by synapses have important functions, while at the same time being highly inadequate to a great deal of information processing.

The need for non-destructive methods of processing complexity

Information must be processed beyond the simple routing methods of the nervous system, and well beyond the rather paltry computing ability of the brain, because so much of data is contextual. The discursion about synapses and their summations was made because indeed it is certain that the traditionally accepted processing methods are crucial to the timing, rhythm, and routing of action-potentials, even while being actually highly destructive of the information within and between nerve impulses. Particularly the contextual information is necessarily lost in a system that sums up disparate knowledge, for downstream there is no differentiation possible for even qualitatively different data.

This problem is no doubt circumvented pre-consciously by the presence of different processing areas in the brain, yet this sort of solution is surely inappropriate in the more general sections of cognition and consciousness. The really substantial problem with imagining the brain to be an analog, digital, or digital-analog computer, is that there is simply no meaning to be had other than the appropriate routing of action-potentials. Information therefore is something that can be processed only as the data have a context of coherent information. The brain cannot process data at all well in an accidental configuration of data in the system of action-potential relays that are merely routing sense responses into motor response because of the loss of informational context in which the processed data essentially exist.

From the lack of intrinsic meaning in the single nerve impulse comes the need to relate information in a manner other than the single and summary methods of simple nerve-synapse processing. The potential effective force of energy differentials across the totality of a set of nerves, no doubt as modified and filtered by summary destruction in the synapses, must be brought to bear on the action-potentials *before* reaching the stage where triggering actions is the primary effect of the nerves. This is in order that the proper "programming", and probably timing as well, might occur *based on the totality of contextual information existing prior to summary and probabilistic judgments at the synapses.*

Information must be processed within its context

Information has therefore to be processed and associated *in situ*. Except for some specialized structures like the neural nets, there really is no other place for data to be correlated (or actually exist) than within the action-potentials as associated sets, along with the fields produced by the action-potentials. And especially, there is no place for quick processing of data, such as exist in the athletics of cats and gibbons, other than via some sort or another of associations which would route the nerve impulses.

The effective force of both new sensory data and recalled knowledge must quickly integrate to themselves and to each other *as effective data*. The coordination and rhythms of the data must become established in circuits that have developed under the influence of similar data, yet which are not fully "programmed" to all possible configurations. Surely the essential fact is that the entirety of information existing in many separate nerve fibers must accurately affect much or all of the information in its "set"[15] of nerve impulses at the same time that the same set is being affected (and it must be done quite accurately) by numerous other nerve fibers. This process is not possible through the summary, duplicatory, and probabilistic collections of capabilities afforded by dendrites, axons, and synapses, let alone is it possible to be done quickly through them.

The sort of medium necessary for lossless information processing

Information held in the differences between nerve impulses within the more general regions of the brain seems able to seamlessly and quite accurately affect and be affected by other such information. Otherwise it would not be useable. The binding problem of information and cognition requires for its solution not only the mechanical operations of synapses and nerves, but a "fluid" medium in which differential information can both exist and interact with little loss. Effectively, a sort of "field" is needed which is finely divided yet able to allow information to propagate across the divisions.

Fortunately there is not much of a problem in envisioning how a field like this might exist, since the electro-chemical operation of the action-potentials coursing down nerve fibers cannot refrain from producing the magnetic and electrical fields which are readily measured in the brain. Obviously, then, it is not surprising that these fields (waves, forces, etc.) exist, nor should it astonish that when in close enough proximity these must also interact. What is needed to bolster the case for electro-magnetic information interaction is to show how it appears inevitable that information exchange must be induced across nerve impulses and how this is evidently crucial for the sake both conserving and of processing information accurately.

Cognition and consciousness deal primarily with differential information being compared, associated, related, and combined in a precise manner that

---

[15] This book often refers to "sets" of nerves and nerve-signals. I am fully aware that there are probably not many truly separate "sets" of data in conscious cognition, although there are probably identifiable groupings. Even if the latter is true, however, the primary reason for writing of "sets" is that it is a convenient, logocentric if you will, way in which to consider a phenomenon that is probably closer to being a continuum.

seems not to occur outside of consciousness. What seems to be the difference in informational states between consciousness and unconsciousness is in fact this ability to bind together and causally affect data within the "stream of consciousness", within a "field" which is unlike the apparently hazy and imprecise forces of the unconscious.

The ability of consciousness to integrate information very quickly across a great number of nervous impulses, as the baseball batter does when subtly adjusting his swing, suggests a quick lateral transfer of information across nerve impulses rather than the simple propagation of a, for example, skew signal into precisely the right nerves. The latter seems too clumsy, too difficult to ensure that the circuitry as well as the information context is just right, especially given our probabilistic synapses. While on the other hand, lateral movement of information through electro-magnetic fields would simply depend on causal transfers within a seamless totality of electrical and magnetic fields.

Fortunately for the argument, the existence of electrical and magnetic forces in the brain would otherwise present us with the problem of the leakage and data, were it the case that these forces could not either be contained or made of some use. Even more auspiciously, this potential "problem" in fact provides the solution to any number of other problems encountered in the operation of the brain—speed and the accuracy of data processing being just two of these.

Chapter 4:

Affection at a distance—harmonics and associations

Our metaphors for mental phenomena apparently came from these phenomena

What is a metaphor? Take the word "resonance" as an instance of a metaphor. What can "resonance" be a metaphor of, except a mental phenomenon considered by us to relate to the "real world"? Or "causality"—a psychological process empirically and rationally fitted via habit to the phenomena we experience. Metaphor, as Nietzsche observed, moves from our experience into a more rationalized and hardened version of our experience.[16] It would not do to pretend that an outside "reality" gave us such beliefs, even though the successful correlations seen in empirical science indicate the usefulness of extending these rationalized concepts theoretically and pragmatically.

So would it be fair to consider a concept like "resonance" as having explanatory value for the operations presumed to exist in mental activity? The fact is that this is probably the role most suited to these concepts formed out of the activities of our minds. "Resonance" should be considered to be a fair metaphor as long it is not understood as a sort of explanation for what occurs "in itself", as if the latter phrase refers to the possibilities of being and knowing. What we could not know is whether or not we know any thing "in itself". What we do know is that we do not feel secure in a belief or idea unless it has some sort of correspondence, "resonance", or the right rhythm. Furthermore, it appears as if something as mysterious as the "hidden attunement"[17] gave us the truths (to the extent "truth" has meaning) of music and mathematics well before causal models existed for phenomena such as harmonies.

Rhythm, electro-magnetic induction, and communication of information

There surely must exist rational "truths" that are not a matter of attunement—and these can be apparently vague cognitively and consciously until a certain kind of reaction to it has developed. However, the usual manner of considering things in full, which is to say deliberation and the like, seems to happen as a conscious meshing of the parts within the cognitive field, and even when we are thinking only lightly, this same process seems to be going on. Since this sort of meshing almost certainly is also essential for an ordered flow of nerve

---

[16] This is particularly the subject in Nietzsche's *On Truth and Lies in the Extra-moral Sense.*

[17] Heraclitus' term, and an important concept in his philosophy.

impulses, the congruent flow of neighboring action-potentials could be thought a candidate for a linking the phenomena of cognition and consciousness. At least this would be the case when the two are simultaneous, a very common although perhaps not invariant experience.

With that introduction leading the way, the matter of the induction across nerve impulses can again arise. The possibilities of electro-magnetic inductions are, of course, well known, induction being what causes transformers to hum. Recently it has been shown that magnetic induction of current in the brain can be about as effective as electrical stimulation. Using either one, some fairly coordinated motor responses can be elicited, but the magnetic method is substantially less painful[18]. However this is produced, it demonstrates clearly that magnetic forces can induce not only actual electrical currents, but action-potentials as well (although it could be the case that action-potentials arise from induced electrical currents, yet even this would demonstrate a causal relationship, albeit one long well-known with regard to electricity).

Not that it is surprising, but this magnetic induction of motor responses indicates that actions apparently have set patterns that they follow when the nerves are triggered. To relate this to the shaping considered in the last chapter, presumably these patterns would under normal autonomous functioning have been tuned by the information processed in the nervous system, into a fairly stable configuration. The sort of induction mentioned above does not, however, indicate much about the fine-scale inductions between nerve fibers that seem inevitable, only demonstrating the possibility of magnetic induction affecting nervous impulses. And these fine-scale inductions would also not be something at all unexpected in the case of electro-chemical impulses moving as action-potentials down the paths of the neurons. Regardless of whether or not the aforementioned gross induction involves electrical currents as intermediates, the possibility of some direct transfer of energy into the electro-chemical phenomenon of action-potentials is virtually a given.

Taking into account the fact that nerve impulses are chemical, electrical, and necessarily magnetic because they are electrical, there are several ways, and combinations thereof, for there to be energy and data transfers, "cross-talk", between nerves. But the best candidate for cognitive and conscious communication across nerves is, of course, the magnetism that has been proven effective for gross stimulation of nerves. The opportunities for fine-grained data transferal are to be found in the intersecting magnetic fields that appear to provide an almost inevitable medium connecting, and providing communication prospects for, adjacent nerves. Magnetic inductions should be thought of as the

---

[18] Hallett, Mark. "Transcranial magnetic stimulation and the human brain". *Nature* v.406 13 July 2000 pp. 147-150/

likely processes providing relatively rapid communication laterally across nerves, while the electrical and chemical effects in and around nerves allow for other communication possibilities as well, though these are not the subject of this book.

There simply is no possibility that when, as seems inevitable, inductions across nerves take place, information will not be transferred. It may be possible that in specialized structures, such as in much of the visual cortex, information is protected from much induction through "codes" and nerve firings that are quasi-digital. Nevertheless, in the more general cognitive and conscious brain regions, where data are associated and bound collectively, there appears to be little chance that substantial inductional transfer does not occur. Let it be duly noted, too, that the sorts of conventionalized limits (like codes) that may be possible in specialized areas would be unlikely to be effective in general associational areas with their relative freedom of association.

No obvious limit could prevent data transfer across a cognitive whole, a mental picture for example, so apparently the information contained within the totality would have to "decide" how inductions would change the whole. All of this would necessarily be contingent on the arrangement of nerves, of course, and rhythm and resonance would depend both on that as well as on the particular configurations of cross-inductive action-potentials in neighboring nerves. And since it is these configurations of action-potentials, along with their relations and differences in respect to each other, that actually contain much of the brain's dynamic information, the sorts of harmonies or rhythms that naturally arise out of interactions would essentially involve data transfers even for these to exist.

Rhythm and resonance thus by their nature require that order and relation, as well as both differentiation and combination, of information exist in the interactions of nerve data. This probably is unavoidable in the "general work space", as some have called consciousness[19]. In addition, these are natural processes for consistently relating the information held across individual action-potentials, since the same harmonies and rhythms will recur as long as the arrangement of nerves stays the same. What probably is usually vital to a system of self-existing information held in and across action potentials is that the resonances that arise correlate well with the energies and forms of the nerve impulse—these together ultimately constitute the information—and often this would mean developing into the large-scale phase synchronizations sometimes seen in portions of the brain.[20]

---

[19] Daniel Dennett's writings are where I first encountered the term, which is not to imply that he necessarily invented it.
[20] Fitzgerald, Richard. "Phase synchronization may reveal communication pathways in brain activity". *Physics Today*. March 1999, pp. 17-19.

Synchronization, resonances, and the like, provide the sort of stable context needed not only for information processing, but also for the continuity of information that depends on the data transfers that occur when the nerve firings come into rhythm and harmony. Fortunately, either magnetic or electrical fields should affect each other with superb accuracy, although it is less clear how these would translate into action-potentials. For our purposes of conceptualization it most likely is enough that this translation is almost certainly inevitable, and in a manner dictated by the physics of electro-magnetism. What matters is that, to the extent that inductions transfer form and substance at all, such a seamless movement of energy and data across magnetic or electrical fields should yield a very good transfer of data. Chemical and mechanical effects would, it must be recognized, be substantially less likely to accurately transfer information between nerves. It may be that interactions such as these are suppressed in preference for electrical interactions, and especially suppressed in favor of magnetic induction.

Resonance and continuity of information

Information flowing undistorted across the divided yet continuous field of nerves as resonances set up ought to be able to produce continuity of information in two ways. The first is that once a resonance is established, data within the collection of action-potentials ought to achieve an enhanced robustness, a resistance to losing the kind of data which might disrupt the rhythm. And the second is that harmonics and resonance provide the opportunity to establish a oneness in discontinuous phenomena. This is most obvious in music, where octaves and fifths are somehow "whole" even though discontinuous.

In the first case mentioned above it is a matter of preserving information, and probably most of all recurrent and patterned information. To do so would likely require data that conforms to a rhythm or harmonic. This means that some data would fit well into the dynamic, some would probably float superimposed on the rhythm (overtones, etc.), and some probably would either be lost as heat or noise or simply distort. So it seems as if the data will predominate if they resonate, or are otherwise somehow congruent. No doubt this should be considered to be quite obvious in music, yet one should also consider that probably a kind of resonance or harmony also shows up in the phenomenon of Gestalts, and when rational thought is felt to suddenly "click".

An important consequence of resonances could be that some of the data losses suffered specifically both in the probabilistic operation of synapses and in the summary processes occurring as dendrites feed data into the synapses, may be reduced by the emergence of resonances which incorporate the data. While this certainly is a considerable conjecture, there is a considerable problem for the survival of information within the bare concept of nerves acting similar to wires coupled via informationally-destructive, probabilistically triggered synapse firings. This problem needs solutions such as this conjecture. At least it may supposed that inductive resonance can play a role in bringing together, and in the preservation of, data that are in a (learned?) manner reciprocally reinforcing, and which thus have the tendency to preserve the information thereby incorporated.

One further probable consequence of the development of harmonies and congruences is worth mentioning. The resonances set up would in this scenario also produce an overall skew, direction, or shape, to the overall sets of rhythms, as dictated by the contextual information being processed through cross-inductions (in other ways too, of course). That is to say, a self-propagating rhythmic whole should tend to preserve this overall information contained within it, even as the information evolved and developed, and this would show up in the direction and shape of the nerve impulses that support the resonances and information during the interaction of these across the nerves.

The hidden attunement and continuity across gaps

The second issue emerging from the proposed phenomenon of discontinuous harmonics nonetheless creating a whole is more interesting, and it may reveal a more important mental process as well. Before Heraclitus, the Pythagoreans were fascinated by the non-causal (as causality was understood) harmonies to be found in the universe, and they believed that *kosmos* exists according to *harmonia*[21], making the concept into sort of a religion. Certainly this is nothing unusual for religions, considering how many religions have held to be sacred various incantations, music, rhythm, and famously the "lost chord". In our time, though, it is easy to forget that many of the "connections" in mathematics, music, as well as in the observable world in general, are not in fact evidently causal or continuous (or are so in fairly recent, relatively high-level, theory). If we were not so familiar with (or bored by) math and music, we might find their power to be "magical" as well.

If harmonies, Gestalts, rhythms, and rational agreement with perception are indeed matters of inductive reinforcement, then there can be an explanation for our perception of discontinuous phenomena as wholes. We do often prefer these phenomena because we perceive them to be pure, whole, and often, "rational". Distortions in the separated "wholes", although these tend to reduce separation, are frequently seen as disturbing and "evil". Why? It is likely that this is because distortion disrupts the mutually supportive inductions that produce harmonics and in that way distortion compromises the strong clear signal needed

---

[21] A source for this and other Pythagorean ideas is: McKirahan, Richard D., Jr. *Philosophy Before Socrates* Indianapolis/Cambridge: Hackett Publishing Company, Inc., 1994. pp. 79-115 especially.

to produce and control the actions for whose creation the brain exists. After all, actions are not in themselves relative phenomena.

The propensity to find the resonant frequencies and strong signals out of a noisy background is evidently a powerful one. A note is due here stating that different mechanisms, including a possible role for synapses, are likely to play their parts. Nonetheless, the fact that there certainly is something potentially uncanny in the Pythagorean realization that musical "wholes" exist according to whole number ratios should alert us to the fact that not only is there a binding problem for the knowledge that exhibits continuity, but also for knowledge that does not. Creative and associational cognition, and the knowledge that "feels right" in spite of no certain connection, provide some of the bases we have for understanding. These capacities constitute a share of the pre-rational resources of the mind.

Recognition of identities through harmonies and resonance

It does seem that there is a kind of self-identity across self-reinforcing yet separate inductions, and not just in continuous information. This is most clearly noticeable in, not surprisingly, octaves, where two separate tone qualia merge in one sense (and not in another) into a single, "same", tone. The resonant overtones in octaves and in other "whole" chords manage to make the overall tone richer, perhaps, indeed, tending to fill in the spaces between notes with overtones and other resonances, even though these leave the actual notes oddly separate still, complete. And in the case of octaves, we know them as "identical". Overtones and resonance apparently involve the brain more, increasing both wonder and inductive complexity, yet thereby emphasizing not the resonances between the notes, but the notes, the tones, themselves, their "wholeness", and again in case of the octave, their "identity".

Thus it seems that the more our perception represents the notes in a chord as *discontinuous,* the greater the chord's purity and wholeness, unless the discontinuities are lessened by resonant tones. In the latter case there is a difficult to describe enhancement of the whole. Apparently consciousness is subtly altered by reinforcements of the pure tones effected by resonance. Indeed consciousness seems affected by the resonances of the tones in chords and octaves themselves, and not simply by overtones, so it may well be that the resonance effect in consciousness is roughly the same phenomenon in either case.

A reason for considering resonances *per se* here, though, is that they are good candidates for being produced phenomenally by small-scale resonant inductions across neurons. On the other hand, chords and octaves seem less obviously the result which would follow from such an easy model of resonant induction[22]. I suspect that octave identities are nonetheless the result of interactions of the resonance that exists between low and high notes, regardless of whether or not these are accompanied by overtones. The resonance of the rich tones of a Stradivarius would seem to lend plausibility to this notion, through consideration of the evidence that the overtones appear to reinforce the separate notes, rather than continuity itself.

It is difficult to conceive of how octave tones, of all things, could remain separate and yet to be counted the "same" except through an inductive resonance that has to be "realized" as similar or same, while at the same time our rational judgment considers the notes to be different. It should be repeated here that what is interesting is that the reinforcing overtones and resonances are not *needed* to fill in the space between the notes of an octave (some of these inevitably occur, yet we can do without them), but rather that the two can support each other across the discontinuous octave.

As pointed out earlier, though, these reinforcing rhythms and resonances should lend stability to information when they do exist, while dissonance tends to result in confusion. On either the larger or smaller scale, resonances and harmonies evidently are capable of producing a kind of unity as well as stability, and thus appear to be good candidates for explaining at least in part the binding problems of cognition and consciousness.

I have used music to exemplify the unities possible through resonant inductions because harmony and resonance are so obvious in music, indeed, the terms associated with resonances and harmonies come largely from music. A caveat must be made—it being that the issue of harmonies does appear less clear in some other senses. Especially in the matters of olfaction and taste it is hard to see clearly where resonance might have an important effect, which is not to deny the possibility. And indeed, these two senses may very well be older, less conscious, and less cognitive than the senses of sound and sight, and thus less dependent on harmonic signals. From experience it seems vision is at least somewhat less reliant on resonance and harmony, though it may easily be that vision is quite dependent on resonance in order to "realize" things, to recognize a "fit". After all, we do have a strong tendency to recognize patterns, and in a related phenomenon, to project familiar shapes onto the visual field. This latter effect brings up the question of how projections may join and "resonate" with sensory data—likely the projection and the sensed data reinforce each other, for which task harmonic reinforcement appears suited. That having been stated, it is

---

[22] Note that I am not pretending any sort of induction to be simple, and am only using a simple concept of what *might* happen in order to discuss some of the possible simple concepts which may underlie what is most likely a highly complex totality.

also true that the quite massive complexity of vision means that it is a less clear example than is hearing for cognitive processing via resonance, presumably resonance operating via induction.

Induced energies and information merging into identities

Whatever the uncertainties in the neural forms taken by data from the various senses, no obvious reasons actually preclude most of cognition from incorporating a great deal of inductive resonance within its ordering and processing of energy and information. And harmonics include certain obvious advantages in that, as in our perception of the octave, these may very well be able to equate the separate and the different without irrevocably merging them. In visual projection this sort of equation would proceed via a self-identical resonance, produced by cross-inductions, between the visual sensory field and the projected form of, for instance, a rabbit. That would constitute a crucial means used in order to identify something like a rabbit.

Possibly the best argument for resonant induction producing identification in the "non-identical" is that action-potentials simply cannot be identical (they can be summed, etc., but do not gain identity in this way), while on the other hand, inductions inherently merge into the identity of the fields which are constituted via induction. Once resonance develops, the mutually reinforcing inductions create a mutually supporting "identity", through the medium of the mutually affective electro-magnetic inductions.

At any rate, it should be recalled that if the fields overlap, as seems evident from EEGs, such fields could not even be prevented from interacting. The only question then is to what extent they interact, and what the magnitude of effect these types of relations have. Important to note here is the fact that if it is the case that neurons parallel each other very far, then the interactions between them would not have to be great at any one point for the total effect to be quite substantial.

In this scenario of fine-scale induction, information in the nerves retains both the fineness and overall unity that we experience cognitively. The binding problems of cognition and of consciousness are therefore possible to solve if this is can be considered to be an adequate model (as far as the model goes, that is). For as long as the environment and genetics provide the conditions that form and situate the nerves appropriately, resonance not only could ensure cross-communication between neurons, but also that nervous impulses do not simply converge into a low-information average. Information can thus maintain its integrity long enough for it to interact, doing so at least into the conscious regions of the mind, and not necessarily losing its coherence until reaching the synapses which finalize and concretize the nerve impulses that produce actions.

Induction hardly accounts for all processing, and synapses probably do even help some to coordinate and synchronize the whole, presumably filtering out some noise, while other synaptic functions might simply be to make adjustments. So most likely there is a role for synapses in processing information as well, even if sometimes synapses, particularly but not necessarily exclusively electrical synapses, in all likelihood merely transfer the signal without much change being effected.

The possibility that this also has something to do with our preference for symmetry is worth mentioning. A collection of nerve firing in inductive resonance is likely to generally have a certain amount of symmetry, however much detailed information exists in its shapes and forms, both internal and external. In important ways it would not be truly symmetrical, yet it seems reasonable that wide-scale induction would tend to spread out the energies of the firings more equally, hence somewhat symmetrically. This is noted here not for its importance to the rest of the model, but simply because it appears that it might have something to do with our tendency to like symmetry and regularity. The advantage of this model is that it allows for a great amount of variety as well.

Associations could result from induction

Arguably, the most useful and important operations of the brain revolve around the possibilities the brain allows for highly fluid associations. I contend in this section that this powerful ability is due to the electro-magnetic inductions in the brain.

Octaves and the other chords are kinds of association, of course. Mathematics, as has previously been implied, may slightly expand the set of possible associations, and these, too, *may* be sometimes due to resonant inductions—although mathematical ability seems to go beyond these. The really impressive capacity for association, however, goes well beyond harmonics and mathematics to provide us with new associations, habitual associations, and the all-important creative associations. None of these three truly belong to the categories of the mathematical or the precisely harmonic.

Certainly the entire matter of induction could hardly be merely about rhythm, harmony, and resonance. These are, rather, important parts of how association might work instead of an exhaustive list of its possibilities. Presumably it is the portions of information that enter into harmonics that manage best to propagate themselves, especially since these support each other. However, undoubtedly the overall configuration of the largely resonant sets of neuronal firings would also bear the crucial information of differing contexts, as would any number of superimposed waves, etc., not to mention the potentials in the fields extending out from the action-potentials.

What is relevant is not especially that information take any particular form, rather that there be the ability to contain and process a great deal of information within a total context which can incorporate the information into its neurons, resonances, and the overall configuration of nerve firings and their associated electro-magnetic fields. And for the sake of maintaining context in this text it should be again called to mind that such a totality would seemingly have to rely on cross transfers, probably via induction, in order to shape output information fast enough for the athletic feats of gibbons and cats. Action-potentials move too slowly to fully integrate new information into cognition for the sake of timely actions, including the rapid visual integrations of which we are capable.

The fineness and the efficiency of inductional information transfer are what permit us precision in our associations of data. That is to say, we need tiny divisions as an explanation of our detailed cognition, another reason why information must be communicated and combined very accurately. The data in output is no doubt less than that in the input, but it can not generally be severely less. Associations must maintain high information content even while they evolve in the process of uniting sets of data. The conservation of data that we apparently experience, even though it exists relatively within our to our minds, seems to indicate that data transfer can indeed occur without heavy reductionism. In other words, association typically develops according to the data within the sets of information that are becoming associated, producing a flexible and changing response driven along to a fair degree by its own information content. Evidently this does not greatly reduce the totality of knowledge even as it finds new resonances and configurations—as long as the data are compatible, that is.

We receive a substantial advantage from the relativistic nature of our associations. The disadvantages had from relativism are also substantial, yet our rationalistic capabilities, perhaps including some derived from the harmonics coming out of our brains, are able to compensate for a good portion of this disadvantage. One of the advantages is the ability to keep the entirety of the information rich, diverse, and capable of new associations, able to mutually transfer information efficiently across the associating data sets. And it allows new information to be placed into a context. Without our free, flexible, and relativistic associational abilities, information would have to be stored, and then compared by utilizing high levels of computation. But in our associational processes, allowing data transfers to leave most of the data in play in the relativistic whole, there is a massive affection in both directions between the associating data sets, as the data interact to produce congruities and also unique combinations of information.

Memory is data-poor in comparison with our rich conscious associations

A major reason to believe that cognitive conscious data are only in existence as they associationally interact is that perceptual detail is rather more data rich than are memories or visual hallucinations[23]. Memory stays the same once in storage, but when it is retrieved it is variable, fluid, and associational, one reason why it is able to support phantom hallucinations. The point here is that though retrieved memories are relatively low in information and therefore all too insubstantial, yet because it is data-poor compared with sensing it must also be as accurate as possible. That is to say, like actions, memory must be made from a whole that includes as much of the relevant information as possible even though it cannot store all of it, for otherwise memories would not be properly constructed. Then it must regain some detail (not the same as that which made it, of course) associationally from the perceptual field as it is taken out of storage and returned to activity in the mind.

For although memory needs to be reliable in the information that it does store, it has few points of reference. It is the whole of whatever associated data sets a memory incorporates that is able to serve as contextual reference for the data complex, and the relative lack of spatial reference gives the memory flexibility in application. The data that make the memory must, as much as possible, exist as an entirety, and the data that relate concept and memory no doubt need to be quite complete as well. This is how we are able to create conceptual maps over time[24], and how we are competent to join them together as well.

The brain is considered to be an analog entity for the most part. But its operational fineness significantly exceeds the fineness of its memory capacity—even as we rely on memory for our operational integrity in the world. Memory is well coordinated in the associations that make it up, produced as it is from the sheer associational relativity of otherwise largely unreferenced data. The only way to create these mostly accurate memories to act as future references for further data-rich actions is to have fine, accurate data relations, such as one might suppose would exist in finely divided fields within which cross-inductions happen.

---

[23]Strong visual hallucinations, with the detail and strength of real vision, are believed not to exist—and of course visual hallucinations are made out of the resources of our mind, such as memory. For a source on visual hallucination, see Dennett, Daniel. *Consciousness Explained* Boston: Little, Brown and Company, 1991.

[24] These maps are, no doubt, also oriented with a rational visual field—it is difficult to think that we could experience anything but a Heraclitean flux (we have that too) without being born with rational capabilities, still the maps themselves have their data oriented to each other (on top of the rational component), associationally for the most part.

Non-causal associations via induction

The need for inductional data interactions across the fine divisions of nerves may also be seen by comparing the brain with human-made analog computers[25]. The latter can accurately follow complex causal relations beginning from simple systems of data, and also are able to incorporate new data according to the same causal patterns. This is nothing like most of the operations in our brains. For as has been observed already, the neuron-synapse system is too inaccurate to account for the actions we perform with precision in our shifting contexts, and our inability to predict the outcomes of the complex relations analog computers seems to agree with this (other causes for this are certainly possible as well, however). We are able to non-causally (that is, without following the chains of causality in phenomena we observe) integrate complex information sets with substantial competence, yet we cannot predict, except very generally, the futures of these systems. Causality must, of course, play a definitive role in our remarkable associative abilities, yet most of the notions that we have about causality are the results of the associations we make (via the non-evident causal moves in the brain). For the most part we do not know causality by modeling it, rather we do so by observing patterns that we associate with their contexts, and particularly through associating different phenomena in the course of time we assume that there is a temporal causality to these phenomena.

The foregoing is one of the most important and essential facts about our nervous system compared to digital and analog computers. We have to *learn* causality from the associations we make, while both analog and digital computers are *predicated* on causal principles. The basic operational causality of brains and of computers are fully opposite, for we relate information before we know consciously how to do so.[26] We can and must learn causal "truths" and causal fictions from informationally rich and largely accurate associations, while computers recreate the associations we make from the causal "truths" and causal fictions that we build into them. What once were the mystical harmonies and congruences of music and mathematics are later reduced to serving the essentially causal ordering of computation, even though the strange associations found in harmonics and in mathematics are sensibly non-causal (or have high-level causal explanations derived partly from what we know non-causally).

---

[25] It may be that other types of analog computers exist, but in my example I am considering the sort I know a little about, analog computers that follow long chains of causality to model the complexity which results.

[26] I am not, of course, denying that operational causality existed in each brain from the very beginning, rather that in most cases we have to learn how to make causal *judgments*.

Once, these were conceptions of what must be true beyond what can be seen, but they also can be causally operative associations.

What we know most certainly, mathematical and logical proofs, are, I believe, associational instead of causal, for it would be impossible to arrive at the answer without rules for association (axioms and postulates, etc.). These are not what we typically consider as associational thinking, but even if they are a special kind of association (which is likely), they are also tools for: associations, as these are generally known. This demonstrates the importance of associations—not that this was in doubt, but it underscores the fact that very much of the brain's capacity is dedicated to associations, with little or nothing giving to us a causality that is not learned. This goes a long way to explaining why it is that humans are truly bad at thinking things through to first causes and first principles, and why they are really good they are at accepting whatever pragmatic reasoning is given to them.

Nietzsche covered this well, especially in *Joyful Wisdom*, so there is little for me to add concerning it except to note that in fact the tendency to herd thought is probably an evolutionary reason for the predominance of associational thought, and not merely a result of it. For associational thought lets herd animals reason according to what the herd thinks, to anticipate and predict what the herd will do without the herd rules needing to be stable or to necessarily be in accordance with the inanimate world (though some rules must agree with the world, naturally).

Still, there is also obvious value in associational thought for modeling what happens in this world of effects and very difficult-to-discover causes. It likewise agrees with the original purpose of nervous systems, with the routing action-potentials and secondarily allowing some of the information (and energy fields) associated with them to shape and to help route the overall set of action-potentials. For example, a sperm whale hunting a giant squid can route to cognitive areas of his brain the sensory impulses perceived of the squid, there to associate disparate data from the senses along with remembered information so that he may accurately shape and direct the response. The whale can do all of this without ever having to consider causation. Back at the whale's mind, the causal force of the energy in which the information resides is being accurately transmitted in an energy field, or in other words in a number of overlapping fields surrounding the neurons. This does occur according to the causal nature of electro-magnetic fields, and not according to the causality of the squid, something that can only be learned over time by us, and perhaps by the whale. These field interactions allow us to "find" associations, and to create new ones, perhaps, indeed, a new configuration for hunting squid. That is to state that we can, through induction, create new causal interactions, ones that could prove very useful in our actions.

This is how we can be creative, how we can dream in a "logic" which is due to "simultaneity in time", as Freud observed[27]. Humans have progressed enough to be able to look for causal associations, but these are really suppositions that we make based on conceptions we have and evidences that actually remain little more than associations arranged by habit[28]. If one thing happens before another we often think that one caused the other—and we believe this assumption to have been only rarely correct historically, at least fundamentally. Pragmatically, however, our causal models have been quite successful, particularly at present, and theories such as quantum mechanics *may* correspond with some of the fundamentals of the universe.

Magical associations

What apparently happens inductively is that, when data sets are associated some of the information from both sets transfers inductively between each other, and this causes changes to the rest of the information in the two sets. And thus is an association born. This shift in information is sensed, perhaps due more or less to information being energized (this remains a big question, though), and the two tend afterward to remain related in our minds. In this very tentative scenario, if one is felt to "cause" the other (without being expected on our part), this would probably be due to the effect of one data set having more force and energy than the other one. However, I would generally expect causality to be nearly equally felt in both, except that commonly a temporal ordering seems to give priority to the earlier over the later. The causal assumptions from temporal ordering would also agree with the concept of greater force seeming to be taken as the more causal, as the developed force of the earlier nerve-firings impacts the incipient force of the succeeding and resultant sets of nerve-firings.

Even in the sort of association being discussed here, the connection we make may appear magical to us. But when the association is considered to be simultaneous, symmetrical, and unconnected, as the Pythagorean conceptions of mathematical and musical relations were, then the associations are able to appear as especially mysterious and magical. Such "sacred" relations (as numerology) showed up in cathedrals long after the Pythagoreans, though it is not clear to what extent they were believed. We, on the other hand, have desacralized math and music through our rules and practical use of them, especially mathematics, but our viewpoint is not the original one.

---

[27] Sigmund Freud. *The Interpretation of Dreams"* 1st part. London, Toronto: Butler and Tanner Ltd., Frome, 1900 (1953 edition) p. 314.

[28] There really is more to it than that, such as unavoidable geometric effects in the space of the visual field, but largely causality is constructed by us—even if reasonably, and with empirical confirmation.

One needs only to consider the powerful feelings of luck, conjunction of circumstance (stars, rituals), and magic, to realize the primeval sense of what causal connections are. The gambling industry relies on the natural expectations that we feel when we make associations in order to give people the feeling that they can win, that they can beat the system. Those taken can experience derision for being deceived by such "unreliable" methods (associations), yet the instinctual associations made by the gambler really are valuable means of knowing. They simply happen to not work where truly random events are occurring, like the ones most gambling machines and games are designed to produce. The gambler "unconsciously" searches for the hidden attunement. If there is one to be found, the human brain has the capacity to make the connection via association of disparate phenomena, and in fact gamblers do in this way often find profitable associations in non-random games.

The reason that dreams are so lacking in "logic" is the same one that indicates to us that the Grimm fairy tales possess a magical truth—most "causal" explanations are actually nothing of the sort. The associations we experience in dreams and in fairy tales are as reasonable as the ones that we mistakenly think are "rational", but are really empirical and pragmatic (usually, anyway). For what we know to be the case has been found out through experience, while dreams fairy tales and free association all permit the process of association to occur without being bound by past learning, valuable though that knowledge may be[29]. In a dream one vision gives rise to another, and the temporal order is naturally taken as somehow causal. In a fairy tale, the fact that words give rise to powerful forces in our minds is taken to be the reality of the world, and so we can easily take an incantation to have the same causal force in the world that it has in our minds. And of course, incantations are little more than associations humans make with sets of objects and actions.

A very important fact comes (associationally) out of these observations. This is that the sense of "causation" (in the primitive associational sense, of course) evidently comes out of the sense that one set of information gives rise to the other[30]. It is, naturally, often assumed that either set could cause the other to appear, perhaps because one association often brings the other out of memory (or otherwise seems to give rise to its perception).

---

[29] It is often thought that our capacity for *logic* is reduced in dreams, and though it may be, it is not as diminished as the many believe, because these people confuse logic with learned associations.

[30] Again, this is why words are thought to be causes—they are, though only as associated in our minds.

Metaphor returns to consideration

Metaphor is again worth some consideration at this point. Just as we deem external harmonies to be "in sync" due to, quite probably, some sort of internal resonance, we also think of things as being "causal" from a very real sense of causal connection—and the metaphor arises because of a real causal force. It is important to recall that, at least according to the hypothesis posited here, associations appear causal not necessarily because they mimic any external causalities, rather because information-energy transfers occur (causally) as cross inductions. The "dependence" that we sense between data sets is real at the time the association is made (because they cause each other), and later it will often be perceived that the rhythms of one are not complete without the complementary and reinforcing rhythms of the other. That is to say, we may sense the lack of context in which the association was made, perhaps because the loss of context distorts the remaining data that depend on it, and our consciousness becomes distorted, energetically incomplete, and non-harmonious—the loss of self-identity may play a part in the sense of distortion and unease, for order and reciprocation would be lost as forms lose energy with no complementary harmonious gain. We *can* recognize distortions, at times anyway, however it is that this recognition happens.

The crucial point about metaphor is that it is associated with our perceptions of certain situations, and the metaphor can associationally give rise to thought of the situation, or the situation can equally cause the emergence of the metaphor. The confused direction of causality surrounding metaphor seems to be internally consistent with this hypothesis, since associations may inductionally transfer data both ways. This is therefore an explanatorily productive model of neural activities, as it provides an account for how it is that we in fact identify a word (or a thought) with a perception. The two evidently have an inductional identity.

Clearly in a way it is true, as Gorgias stated in classical Greece[31], that words cause thoughts and feelings in the hearer. It is nonetheless hardly a straightforward causal process, instead being a complex associational phenomenon, as anyone who has sought to persuade or seduce knows. It seems that if the word "causal" has any significance, it must be self-identical with the psychological sense that makes the causal judgment appear, which is to assert that we must take association to be causal if causality can be consistently derived from associations. To repeat this important step of the argument, the causal judgment must in fact be caused by causally effective associations if our sense of causality has any meaning whatsoever. For we do in fact depend on the belief that associations cause other associations in our very capacity of judging

---

[31] In his *Praise of Helen*

39

causality. Obviously a formal syllogism could be made out of this line of thought, though I will not do it. The raw sense that one concept demands a concomitant as an effect is an essential connection in our being able to decide that one thing causes another thing.

Summary

So this may again suggest the model of inductional associations producing conceptual associations in general, and causal associations in particular, which in turn insists that neural associations are causally linked, and preferably in the partially self-identical manner of interacting cross-inductive fields surrounding neighboring neurons. These would inevitably cause rhythms and resonances to materialize. And in fact it is the mutual harmonic causal reinforcement producing a sort of identity of notes in an octave that is one of the best candidates for an example of simultaneously causal forces acting across two disconnected signals. The probabilistic nature of nerve firings, as well as the information-destroying summations that occur across synaptic structures act in an opposite manner to the apparently information conserving and perceptually dependent associations which are so prominent in our thinking. Out of these opposing processes available to the brain the inductional model of affection may be seen as the more viable explanation for the accuracy with which the brain operates.

Induction has the advantage of providing an account for both the accurate and inaccurate causal assumptions humans make, as well as for the mysteriously disconnected yet crucial knowledge of hidden attunement across resonant phenomena in, especially, audio phenomena. Thus the inductional hypothesis simplifies the explanation of the human brain, but much more importantly, it also unifies cognition by explaining two different types of knowing via a single underlying information processing phenomenon. Thus it binds together two crucial ways of processing information into a process that associates both in a whole. This is a substantial achievement for any cognitive model.

Chapter 5:

Simultaneity of causality and consciousness

The question posed of whether causality can be disentangled from consciousness

Induction is not the only phenomenon which coincides with both harmonic distance and associational dependency. The second phenomenon involving the latter conditions is the one through which the these are realized to exist, consciousness. The normal way in which we know of the "identical" nature of the notes in an octave, and the method by which we sense that associations belong to and complete each other, is the property of consciousness. This barely suggests that the effect of separate data sets on each other within the cognitive realm may have something to do with consciousness itself, yet it begins the argument for it.

A substantial question in regard to consciousness is the manner of the relationships of the various data within consciousness. The (largely) one-way movement of causality in the outside world is not, as many have noted, something readily discerned by the brain. But what is ignored by the critics of causal notions[32] is that the simultaneity of cause and effect in much raw mental phenomena is (apparently, at least) what makes us able to think from effect to cause, and thus able to come up with the thought of cause producing effect. Additionally, this simultaneity probably is what allows for atemporal rational judgments to be effected, including the important, if logically uncertain, judgment of identity. Without these causally ambiguous, yet powerful abilities, the plausible and highly valuable causal chains that we invent or discover would not be available to our minds.

However, the causal, as well as the other forms of dependence, rely on the prior "judgment", or more likely, perception, that there is a dependency between two data sets. Whether or not this sense is always, or even ever, "true", is not at issue here. What matters is that associations and their derivatives like causal judgments are fully established on the sense or "realization" that one concept, mental picture, or "data set", is dependent on another, that both are dependent on each other, or on the uncanny feeling that two things must be connected but one is not sure how so.

---

[32] Currently deconstructionists are the prominent examples of intellectuals that at least ignore causality as traditionally conceived. Their roots are at least partly in Nietzsche and Hume, as well as other philosophers.

Importantly, this feeling of dependence apparently underlies causal notions (or causal *dependence*), as opposed to the sense of causation originally underlying the concept of dependency. Therefore, the apparent, or at least unavoidable, presumption would be that whether in part or in whole, dependency associations also underlie the idea that there is mental causation. So we reach the conclusion that either mental causation and dependency associations share at least a partially identical basis, or mental causality is an invalid concept. This conclusion not, however, written to be taken as anything more than a suggestion, and as an example of the gruesome logical and causal difficulties that we face when it is the basis of the mind that is in question.

So far this chapter has been largely re-stating and expanding on parts of the last chapter. This is because not only do causal judgments need evidence of having a dependence on associations, but they also require a reason to believe that the two are, as suggested above, identical in important ways. Ergo, the realization that one association led to another is considered by us to be mental causation because it is also the relationship that we mean by the term "causation"—seemingly the recognition or extrapolation that within our brains a dependency over time exists. What I am attempting to communicate is not only that our causal assumptions demand the recognition that dependence of one data set upon another over time is our original conception of causality, but also the point that it is the experience of associational dependency through time that gives us the derived, objective, idea of causality. And if our conclusions about causality are correct, they depend on the associations having been causal, for the premise must contain the conclusion. Hence, within the phenomenal realm, we appear to be justified to assume that associations are causal effects, at least those occurring over time, since it is exactly these sorts of associational realizations for which the term "causation" was coined, and from which the causal concept was developed[33].

This argument is being made here for the previously given reasons, but also in order to sidestep questions of whether or not the causal and associational beliefs we have are accurate portrayals of our mental processes, or rather of the "real world".

---

[33] I must note here that not all associations, not even all time-dependent associations would necessarily have to be causal *if* our conclusions of causation are correct, but only the associations that produce causal beliefs would have to be causal. Inductively though, if we lack a reason to believe that the associations not leading to causal beliefs are of a different kind, and all we have to go on is that some have been extrapolated into causality which once had not been, we would generally feel justified in supposing that causality is a general factor in association.

The above-mentioned question is especially inappropriate, since the "real world" that we know is the poorly-defined realm of translation of brain operations into thoughts. It is enough for here and now that we have to consider mental phenomena as having causal effects in much or all of associational thought, simply because that is all that we can mean when we claim to have deduced causal effects out of the associations that develop over time. There is really no way humans can ask what causation means in itself (even though the words can obviously be written), so we only mean by the term "causation" what this means to our minds (whatever that is). For, if one says that such and such a conclusion—quark theory perhaps—is inevitable from considerations in physics, this statement has only to mean that one's mental workings have inevitably caused the effect (this conclusion) within one's brain.[34] And whether or not this conclusion is "true", this is, in fact, what we mean by stating causal judgments.

Proposed exceptions to the evidence that causality takes place in the mental sphere are not difficult to find, for instance, opposites giving rise to each other or uniting into symbols of transformation. We typically assume that causality works even in these cases, but for the present, and indeed most of this book, these as yet unsubstantiated assumptions regarding phenomena that have been mentioned but not given a possible explanation are to be noted, then ignored for the present. These are apparently different processes than the causal processes under discussion, and they may or may not affect the causal and other associational relations that we experience. That is, there is no reason to actually think that any "non-causal" processes normally interfere with ordinary experiences of causality.

So does causality cause consciousness?

What matters is that causality appears mentally to be a derivative of associational dependence. And, as Nietzsche noted in a somewhat different context, this can happen quite independently of any essential causal connections outside of us.[35] Other associational perceptions are likewise considered by us to

---

[34] Obviously here the brain is considered to be the realm of "mental activity", as it appears to be the case according to both common sense and science. Most other ideas about how we perceive and think would not significantly change what is said about psychological causality, however. Those who believe in the "spirit" also speak of causes, while the Homeric world invoked the gods as perceived causes of mental effects (and this perception itself caused effects). Only the working out of cause and effect differs between the brain model and these others, and not the condition, shared by all, that the perception of associational dependence over time is the same as the perception of causation, and is the "cause" of the concept of causality.

[35] Such as in *Beyond Good and Evil*, section 21

be caused, and are therefore probably caused to the extent that we know and can mean something by "cause" (unless this perception, or judgment, were to occur by analogy instead of originally). This raises the question of whether or not consciousness itself would be separate from causality, or is causality simply consciousness, or as I would prefer to think of it, is consciousness really a form of causality? This is an identity question, asking whether or not the two are the *same* thing, not the mindless question of whether or not a cause, or causes, do "cause" consciousness.

To be sure, consciousness is probably not **just** causality. There are the questions of opposition, for instance, and the possibly related matter of potentials existing between differences. Then again, causality is a relatively meaningless term when it is shorn of context, especially once questions of informational interaction and induced energies are considered. Yet, causality is a meaningful general category to us, and the relationships of time-dependent associations are the sort of things of which we are conscious, so it seems appropriate to consider causality as a bare concept on its own before moving on to questions of what mental causality could be like.

At any rate, whatever the status of these questions, a good deal of consciousness is apparently quite involved in the sorts of associations posited in this book to be causally related (as most brain and mind researchers believe), and induction appears to be a reasonable medium for this causation. In our conscious experience we seem to be aware of things that potentially have an effect, and when the effective force of what is conscious seems to disappear (which is to say, if it seems no longer of consequence), that part of consciousness tends to fade out of awareness.

It is true that, although we often retain a memory of causal sets of data, in our normal experience we typically no longer retain consciousness of the data and perceptions that yielded a desirable effect or action once this conclusion has been reached. Consciousness follows quite closely the chains of mental causation (to the degree we can know this), and it, far more than memory does, contains the finely detailed holistic pictures and other sensory integrations that would be capable of producing a precise effect from precisely integrated causal data. This is no new or surprising observation, yet it seems that little has been made of the fact that consciousness of the details which need an accounting in the processes of the brain may in fact be primarily of what consciousness consists.

The conscious field is sometimes thought of as being primarily a play of differences, especially by deconstructionists. If this is probably not the whole of the matter, the sharp and swift focus we place on differences (especially in vision) suggests that this observation does have value. One way to understand these differences[36] is that the accounting for the data (differences in particular) crucial to the causal functioning of the brain shows up in consciousness, and this tends to be what is communicated to the other conscious, language-understanding, beings. So it would seem that both the causally important differences, and the actual sense of the dependence of associations which are also crucial to causal notions, are indeed conspicuously conscious factors. Why, though, do we tend to think that differences and causality are represented in consciousness, and not simply that they are consciousness?

This is not the place for a lengthy discussion of logocentrism and our tendency to think and speak in a manner that insists on the truth of words and the reality of logical judgments whether or not this "truth" and this "reality" are actually "real" (whatever that means). Suffice it to point out that being conscious of something has historically been considered to be the same thing as reality—a probable reason for why dreams and the gods were so often taken to be real.[37] Considered historically, there is thus no reason to think that consciousness of the factors underlying causality is not the same as the working out of causality as it exists as a mental perception. In other words, if a god I perceive makes me do something, is not this mental perception causing my action in very fact?—and this would be true whether or not the god is "real". Notice that this is not the same as saying that consciousness is identical with the *concept* of causality, rather it is to state that this concept relies on perceptions which would have to be consistent with the pre-conceptual components of mental causality, if causality can in fact be said to work in mental operations.

We must in this context consider again the important problem that integration in the brain has—that there simply is no reference against which the data can be compared, like there is in digital and analog computers. Let it be noted that this is not a claim that there are *no* references, since vision clearly has framing elements (even though even these are probably partly set by perceptions), rather it is that conscious differences and sensed dependencies often are plainly relative to data that are not rationally comparable. Consciousness seems to be keeping track of the forms and intensities of causality in its realm, it would seem because there are no (other) references to which data may be related.

---

[36] This is not the deconstructionist interpretation.

[37] I do not believe that ancient man entirely conflated consciousness and reality as some have suggested. Our ability to reason is a crucial faculty existing to resolve the conflicts that pure perception tends to raise. However, the resort to reason appears to have indeed been less common in earlier humans, and the acceptance of the senses and mental experience was simpler, more naïve, and less rationalized.

The only reference against which causality takes place in the overall field is the field itself

Mere nerve firings do have their own references within the nerves, and do not seem likely to react directly to differences, due to the operations of synapses as summary gates (the caveat is that much remains unknown about synapses, though this statement appears true enough at present in regard to most combinatorial synapses). Unknown interactions and novelties, as may appear in the mixing of two data sets inductively, must affect each other accurately without the preset cause-effect relations and reactions of digital and analog computers.[38] One may think that in fact a reference also has to exist for consciousness, and this probably is true. Probably, though, the "reference", such as it is, consists in the totality of the inductively interacting energies. Against that collective reference, the shapes and intensities of the effective energies cause an acceleration[39] of the total energy field. Necessarily, an accounting is made while the data are integrating into the whole, and *that* accounting of causal form and magnitude appears to us as our consciousness.

This "acceleration" is not precisely what is thought of when that term is used in mechanical operations, not even with the caveats made in note thirty-nine, for this acceleration includes the inductive "impact" which maintains the fine forms of the causal links that are possible in tiny overlapping electrical and magnetic fields. The word "acceleration" is used to emphasize that this *is* an energy transfer, one which must register the shapes and intensities of the changes in the connecting fields relative to the causal forces from the differing but joined energy fields. This acceleration (or set of accelerations) is registered by the only thing that can actually embody and contain the information involved in its causality, and this is the changing state *within* the set of overlapping energies of dynamic action-potentials and their associated energy fields.

---

[38] Analog computers are less set in the way they act than are their digital counterparts, yet generally there are not category violations made in them, as there are in our own mental processes, which mix vision and smell, emotion and rationality.

[39] I am using "acceleration" here as it is employed in physics, it being either an "acceleration" or "deceleration" as these terms are used in the vernacular. I adopt the physics definition to this extent because consciousness likewise probably does not discriminate much between the two. Physics also, however, considers acceleration to be change in direction, but I would think that the direction in the nerves is all that matters, as nerves may act largely as one-dimensional conduits to nerve impulses (which are themselves energetic, but are not energetic streams of material such as electrons, for example, so they would not necessarily follow the inertial laws that electrons do), and only reversal of direction would perhaps be experienced as a directional acceleration.

Consciousness registers the account of mental processes

Here is one of the most essential factors at issue in the matter of consciousness—that what we have in our consciousness is the process, not (generally) the final results. This is not the case with logic and mathematics, which suggests that these in fact play a role in providing references points to supplement, and partly make rational, the reference that we have in the entire interacting electro-magnetic field. However, logic and math apparently *are* conscious results of unconscious processes, which as such enter into the larger processes of conscious causality. We seem not in fact to know the ultimate results (for what does one know about typing the words for a book, or how one really makes any movement?), and instead we know how to achieve results. We do, however, become adept at knowing how to channel a combination of emotions, perceptions, and memories into a desired output, that is, we consciously combine causes (or more likely, we are conscious of the combinations of causes) to produce appropriate effects.

At this juncture we must again consider that we know information in conscious detail that seems to exist causally and generally not otherwise. We do not remember the full resonance of the violin even as it plays back accurately and even beautifully in our minds. Understandably, a full memory of tone and resonance, and of all of the shades of color and shadow, would be entirely too much to remember. It is this "lost" information which can explain the difference in richness between sensory experience and the rest of the information in the brain. For, the fullest, richest, and by far the most complex mental phenomena are not the processes of data input from the brain's memory or rational processes, they are rather the relations and syntheses of the information contained in sensory (and other) input.

It is of these latter phenomena that we are conscious. We are aware of the precise differences that show up in the conscious and the causal, and as far as we know, not anywhere else at all. This makes sense if consciousness exists as the causal force of differences which become knowledge accessible to mental processing only *as* differences in relating data. And these differences become related when the information is no longer restricted to the mere data encoded in action-potentials (and series of action-potentials) but when the slight differences between adjacent nerve firings become "known", that is, causally active.

This knowledge of difference (and of similarity, though difference usually is, it seems, the more useful) between discrete information streams enormously increases the working data, of course. In the digital computer the extraction of this information and its use requires a great deal more processing power than we have been shown to possess. Or, in an analog computer the differences work mutually and relative to each other to produce results that have to be interpreted by humans who recognize the "causal" differences in both the input and the results. Digital computers, more than their analog counterparts, are constructed in order to process data according to human interpretations of logic. That being duly noted, the odds that there is a "processor" in our brains that extracts differential information from sensory input and feeds this into the consciousness appear to be very low, since this processor would have to be far more complex and rigidly referenced than consciousness itself. And in fact, the differences have to become effective within the consciousness anyway if our conscious interpretation of experience is to have any reliability. This conscious interpretation is all that is available to our experience in any event.

The disappearance of causal data from cognition and consciousness

So it is that differences show up in their force and their effect within the causal conscious sphere of the mind, and there is nothing to distinguish our awareness and the effect of differences in our minds. This would be *prima facie* evidence that these are the same thing, but there are better reasons to think so. The simple fact that much conscious detail is important in reaching an appropriate action, yet then disappears beyond recall and persistence, suggests that it is conscious only when it is acts as a set of causal phenomena, during which time it creates the proper form and strength of nervous output. After that, much of the detailed information apparently no longer exists.

Or perhaps, to consider it more basically, much conscious detail seems to merely exist as causal accelerations across mutually interacting fields surrounding the neurons. Because it is contextual information[40], and interacting according to temporal information of the sort that is poorly reflected in our memories, it is thus capable of being causal/conscious without being generally susceptible of re-creation in our minds. Not surprisingly, by focusing in on it, the information can be more directly represented in the nerve firing themselves, and other data then become "incidentally" active across the set of action-potentials. However, this "incidental" information is far from being incidental *to the process*, and in fact these data help to ensure the accuracy of the memories and the relationships possible between memories and other brain data, in addition to its role in relating present-time sensory data.

---

[40] This information not only is contextual by being a part of the whole, but also as interactions peripheral to nerve signals. This is probably another reason why it is so causally known—because it is not embodied in the interior of the nerve impulse, its existence makes itself known only through causation.

Mental causation and consciousness are necessarily the same process

What is vital about the whole question of causation in the brain is that to experience it consciously in an at all accurate manner it simply must be the causal process and not merely the "consciousness of" the causal process. This appears to be evidenced by our experience of the simultaneity of decision and commencement of action in most instances. However, the issue that strongly suggests their sameness, is the by now familiar observation that the impact, the accelerations affecting each other, have no reference outside of the context of the set of nerve firings and their cross-affections.[41] Nothing at all can fully transmit or translate all of the knowledge that is interacting at a given time, because it would siphon off some of the mind's causal force to do so.

And if, to get around the siphoning of data, the set of information were split into a causal half and a conscious half, the two would necessarily diverge in their development unless the information had already been homogenized—as it clearly has not been in consciousness. That is to say that although information could be split and still perhaps be enough data for causation and for consciousness to exist well enough, it could not be split into identical halves except by an outside knower. Nor could development proceed in exactly the same way even if the halves could made be identical, for there is noise, randomness, and entropy existing in the brain. So that, since mental causality and consciousness do coincide in regard to information processing and development, therefore the two necessarily are the same process.

Splitting the information is the only conceivable possibility for precise, accurate causality and a finely divided consciousness to be different things, since adding or subtracting energies to consciously "observe" what is happening in causal sections would hopelessly distort the causal chains in the brain. It may be argued that if everything were set up correctly and extremely precisely, there could be a phenomenal consciousness that would be unlike the causal processes, if the phenomenal consciousness drained off carefully controlled quantities and forms of energy. But clearly this is impossible in a nervous system that can handle novel information, indeed, which is heavily shaped by perceptions that once were novel. For in novel situations, the right amount of energy and information to be drawn off could not be known to the process that did this. What really is impossible for our flexible processes of dealing with information is to be able to duplicate or to split the complex processes of analog causation

---

[41] This is probably not exactly true, because there are rational referents, and rationalistic "grids" regulating, for instance, the internal "screen" on which we visualize. But the particular episodes and scenes are not referenced beyond these and a few other possibilities, except through perceptions, memories, emotions, and the other learned and unconscious referents.

that we consciously experience.[42] And, if we are conscious of the complex of causation, then causation is necessarily part of consciousness.

Nevertheless, saying that consciousness is inductive causation can be more than stating the not overly radical idea that causation is conscious (actually, though, the opposite statement is more radical, and this book is claiming it). Inductive mental causation unites the Heraclitean flux (or stream of consciousness) with at least a number of non-causal (in the conventional sense) associations that we readily make—most clearly in the matter of harmonics and spectacularly so where identities in octaves are recognized. Typically we have split apart the stream of consciousness from the simultaneous judgments of sameness and difference in the octave. We have done so especially because we "explain" musical relations according to what does seem to be a separate capacity from streaming consciousness, logic and rationality. Unfortunately, while the logical science of mathematics can describe musical arrangements, it can hardly explain the (synthetic?) identities that we consciously perceive across intervals.

If, however, we are aware of the unities of chords and octaves because the notes do in fact partially cause each other across the interval between them, and we are also conscious of this "unity" simply because it is being produced and caused in this inductive fashion, we can understand that other associations could be made by a similar method. For it is said that we look for patterns in the world around us, and presumably these, too, manage analogously to reinforce each other within the brain, harmonically and otherwise. This could really only work through inductions or something like them, for synapses seem more fitted to filtering out noise than of accurately reinforcing or relating sensory data.

The filtering function of synapses

Synapses, then, probably have two main functions besides summation and replication: the transmission of action-potentials, and the destruction of randomness and noise. Strong signals, and harmonics, end up inductively reinforcing themselves. Weak signals and noise are lost either in the probabilistic operation of synapses or in the summary activities of synapses and are thus filtered out. In this way, the chaotic portions of partly ordered, partly chaotic, patterns that are so common in nature can be taken out, leaving the pattern. On the other hand, since data that are not fully compatible must be given a way to reinforce each other, the capacity for inductive propagation across neurons yields an ideal method of re-creating the identities, though in different form, that presumably produced the patterns originally.

---

[42] The process may be re-created in some manner. It can be redone well by re-perceiving nearly the same sensations, or redone in a significantly poorer way by memory, which has lost a large portion of its dynamic information.

Conscious knowledge of identity and causation from the inside

The identities we "recognize" in octaves and in patterns are known to us from the inside. At least this is how we experience it, and since ideas and concepts of something like the "inside" are produced from such experience, the questions of whether or not our concept of the "inside" is "true" appears to be beside the point here. This manner of knowing identities is a very different sort of knowing than is rationality, something Hegel, and Nietzsche following him, failed to fully recognize. Nietzsche rightly noted that we cannot know anything to be equal, since nothing is so[43], skirting the fact that we do "know" such equalities nonetheless. We know that an "identity" is established in our minds, and this occurs, I believe, by the causal convergence of inductive overlap in the fields surrounding the neurons. It does not matter that we do not know "true" equalities, since we can indeed recognize these equalities in perceptions once two or more have mutually caused each other and at least partially merged into an identity.

The inside nature of the recognition of identities leads, as noted previously, to mystery and the mystical when neither the habitual relation nor the causal force is recognized. How do we know what we know, when no connection is obvious? Because we have no inborn knowledge of chords and octaves, the recognition of their unity has no genetic explanation (at least not in full). Heraclitus' hidden attunement it is. Yet we evidently can know it because there is an inductive causal unity causing the consciousness of sameness, of identity even within clearly demarcated differences.

We are able to see more clearly the inside causal knowledge where the associations are not simultaneous (in a way, though, they are simultaneous while associating), but successive. A caveat should be made here, which is that these mental causes are not what we would scientifically call causes, rather they are simply the phenomenal differences which in our experience give rise to conscious effects and shape motor output. Or one could put it that we sense the shape and force of causation phenomenally, while the true inductive causal links are inferred by us only because we know how to make the right phenomena appear (primarily via the senses, or through memory). Physical causality is a special case of this broader mental causality, in that it is consistently repeatable and it follows logic as it *defines* inductively known empirical rules and facts.

Our conscious ability to recognize mental causality as it consciously shapes results (whether logic is being applied or not) *from inside* of the mind's causality is what really shows of what consciousness consists. This is why the case for

---

[43] *The Gay Science*, section 111

inductive causality had to be made first, in order to show how consistently it accords with consciousness.

Unfortunately, it can be argued that this is not the way in which we normally think. However, the logical and habitual ways of "normal" thinking are the shortcuts that conscious learning creates, that is, conscious realization of inductive force does over time create routes that no longer become conscious to any real extent. So driving becomes largely unconscious in our actions of steering, etc., while perceptions continue to become conscious (if not generally put into memory) in order to shape what have become reflexive actions. This is not the place for lengthy discussions of how actions become habit and reflex, only it had to be pointed out that logic and habit actually seem to be shortcuts around consciousness, and the no longer necessary cognition. This is why a sleepwalker, who is probably at least mostly unconscious, can perform habitual actions while at the same time only poorly integrating new information.

Non-formalized thought, on the other hand, does demonstrate causal force from the inside, as when dreams[44] make direct causal links between successive events, or when late at night one is not sleeping but visual images are shifting within one's consciousness. Then the mutual and quantitatively non-equatable effects show themselves to be consciousness (for that moment) as the causal shifts occur between differing data sets. Then one part of the visual field changes simultaneously with the one with which it is associated. No continuity of either image is assured, and one may completely disappear in causing the other. In fact, over time the disappearance of one is virtually assured, as is the eventual disappearance of the other. And, here too, it seems that causality can operate at distances between visual objects. This seamless change, whether or not there is ever "contact" between associations, makes up the conscious flow, at least when we are in this state. And the conscious flux so experienced in fact seems to serve as a kind of account of and for the changes that are occurring within the consciousness as information interacts.

"Real" causality is merely the derivative of mental causation—and of consciousness

The objection could easily be made that the "real" causality (presumably, this would be causality "in itself") is not a part of our experience, which no doubt is true. However, what would the "experience of real causality" be? Even the mental event has no "in itself" to be perceived. Our internal experience is as close as we come to sensing raw causality as possible. And in this internal

---

[44] I, like many, consider dreams to be a kind of consciousness. This holds true especially for the lucid dreams that occur when one is waking up—indeed awake—but largely ignoring rational cues.

experience, we are conscious of the stream of effects across mutually interacting information sets, *including* the perception of impacts as these are felt downstream from causes. That we orient chains (or webs) of mental causality partly according to the perceived impacts in order to achieve goals provides evidence that consciousness to at least a great extent, coincides with the effects of a comprehensively interacting collection of causal forces within the brain.

The foregoing appears to agree with the observation that we seem most conscious of the information that interacts causally according to **difference**, probably inductively, rather than of the unproblematically routable information (via neurons and synapses) of habit and of the unconscious. After all, even the latter is known via its causal impact within conscious perceptions, even if this is often mysterious, and the associations are not obvious.

To conclude this chapter, it must be stressed that there could be no constant knowledge of causal process in its effects if consciousness were not somehow synonymous with the causality of the mental process. *The observer effect would distort mental causation were consciousness not the same as mental causation.* We are aware of the intricacies produced in the dynamics of mental causality (if phenomenally) as the process happens, and we are particularly aware of the crucial differences which make themselves known through cause and effect. Moreover, we primarily understand mental causation as associational because it is not, in fact, limited to the linear chains of cause and effect in logically constricted processes, as are digital computers.

Causation as we experience it consciously is instead open-ended, driven by the often novel differential data we take in, and causation is mutually interactive across parallel data sets. It is this simultaneity of causation and consciousness that allows us to create the conscious causal models of reality that repeatedly work, and yet which permit us to shape and route action-potentials in order to conform to changing conditions.

Chapter 6:

Induction as a method of internalization

Effects of higher dimensional movements on one-dimensional streams

De Saussure and Derrida proposed that meanings of words are produced in languages via differential effects operating within the entire context of these languages. I have used this sort of language model to partially analogize what I believe happens in the causal operations of consciousness.[45] I wish, however, to make it clear that I did not derive the idea from them, or really anybody, and cite them for two reasons. First, because of the effectiveness of the appeal to authority for receiving a hearing. And second, since I have on my own come to similar conclusions in regard to certain physical systems (if mostly in reverse), I believe that some of the concepts of deconstruction and like theories can be integrated into other philosophies, and even science.

For quite some time I contemplated the forms of beauty existing between order and chaos, forms produced precisely by order's plunge into chaos. Incense smoke, for instance, breaking into mysterious and exquisite shapes, while remaining intact and internally linear. It is true that, once complete chaos arrives, there is no longer any order, little beauty generally, and certainly no beautiful *forms*. However, what is very interesting is what comes prior to that chaotic state, the softening order within a still-intact stream, and the dimensions of causality that begin to act beyond the one-dimensional causality that originally existed (effectively). While the stream continues to move in its essentially one dimension, side forces in other dimensions begin to act, as it were, as differentials in the parts[46] of the one-dimensional stream. Thus randomly (as seen from outside), yet in full accordance with causality, both the one-dimensional flow and the side movements begin to affect each other simultaneously.

---

[45] There are great differences between what I propose for consciousness and what Saussurian and Derridean theory, especially the manner and effects of causation. Essentially causation for Derrida is mechanical and external (except for his mysterious "trace"), while I believe much causation in consciousness to reach straight into the interior, which does not, however, ensure any more accuracy in communicating meaning.

[46] To say "parts" is to speak of arbitrarily divided portions.. Also, "differentials in the parts" is as considered within the stream, for one could as easily think of the asymmetrical overall form which naturally dictates differing internal flows in order to conform internally with the exterior.

A legitimate way, certainly, to think about the foregoing could be that at some point incense smoke begins to move in effectively two or three dimensions rather than in one. Physically there is nothing wrong with that interpretation, in fact this interpretation seems best. But if this sort of phenomenon is thought of as an analogy of the movements and cross-causality of nervous impulses, then the first interpretation given in this chapter best models the effectively one-dimensional movement of action-potentials as they are additionally affected by side forces. These side forces being embodied in the brain by, of course, the cross-inductions that would seem to be inevitable effects in electrical phenomena. Notably, again it is the brain that must understand the forms it perceives, either as they slide from order into chaos, or during their persistence on the edge between order and chaos. And this is important to understanding what the brain does, for these types of forms are actually common in nature.

Cognition must process a great many chaotic, even scattered, forms

The importance of these chaos-softened forms cannot be exaggerated, for the context of reality is substantially made of them. The rational forms also are critical, to be sure, particularly the movements of animals and objects, but these also exist against a backdrop of the artifacts and flow of the Heraclitean flux. Order softens and disintegrates in nature, unities lessen and sometimes merge with what were other unities in a never-ending process. Partly to distinguish these sorts of forms from the purposive movements of animals, the brain must be able to model them in some manner or other. The capacity of understanding, and even of predicting to some degree, the partially entropic forms shaped by water and wind presumably operates in conjunction with our abilities for "free association", since the chaotic is mostly unpredictable. However, this sort of mental operation is probably not all that different from the process of fully integrating any normal scene with which we are presented, as will be argued somewhat later.

Our more impressive talent, however, is in perceiving the sameness of forms that are no longer fully intact, indeed, which may be very much divided. These may be tree branches or the effects of wind in the grass, to name just two. The more beautiful sorts of these forms are the most purely formed, without some defect, or "evil" to "mar" it. Beauty is the measure that we have to distinguish forms that grow well from those that grow poorly, and this includes organisms. Plants are especially vulnerable to deformation by environmental defects over time, and are significantly affected by winds if they are land plants.

But whether the objects are wind-shaped trees, incense smoke, flames, clouds, rivulets, vortices, the erosional features of a landscape, or the rippling of a field of wheat under a gust of wind, certain artifacts of the shaping energy show up when conditions are ideal. These include waves, harmonics, standing waves, chaotic attractors, and similarities altered subtly by slight, if cumulative, differences. Unsurprisingly, a major reason for integrating these "divided unities" is to be able to notice when something disturbs this natural "order", for instance when predators or prey make vegetation move differently than when the wind alone is acting on it. If we could not integrate, more or less, the context of a landscape with wind in it, we could not very well detect danger and opportunity within such an environment.

Visually, harmonics in all probability do have a role in such integrations. The reason that harmonics are so prominently noticeable in acoustics, though, is that sound lends itself very well to producing overtones and, of course, harmonics, and besides, these are what show up in our perception as unities in sound. In the matter of vision, too, the unity of forces acting across vectors needs to be recognized by the organism, sometimes when only continuity can assure unity, sometimes when there exists a unity without continuity. In the case of visual integration of divisions, there has to be a similarity in the overall vector, of course, and then for the differences from the vector to be unified in spite of their individual differences. While this is sometimes effected according to harmonics, probably more often it occurs through the unified actions as a causal whole in our cognitive-conscious processes.

Dynamic causation unifying mental objects and patterns

Although in previous chapters I have mentioned that causality in consciousness has only the whole context as reference, here we must consider more thoroughly the fact that it is also inescapably a shifting context for what is changing[47], despite its including some factors of continuity. Were the context to shift without causality acting in its entirety (in the entirety of the conscious "in focus" region, at least) there might be a conscious impact registered, but there might very well not be a "consciousness of" the scene. By contrast, it is the "artifacts" of the changing scenery, such as patterns and objects, that become conscious wholes as causality works across, through, and according to the entirety of changing differentials. This is as it must be in order to fully integrate the scene with any sort of accuracy, as has been previously mentioned. Here it must be emphasized that while the nerves are divided and relatively fixed, the interactions across these which shape and refine the nerve impulses are simply dependent on the causal forces fluidly interacting with and according to

---

[47] That is, the context is shifting as it becomes integrated into the form that will trigger a response to the situation. It may certainly hold steady, as our perception attests when we continue to look at the same thing for a while, but that itself is done in order to subtly alter and refine the scene, including the context (since that is to what anything within the scene refers), by providing more sensory data of the object.

themselves. There apparently are mental processes, then, that can mimic the causal unities of partly chaotic phenomena. And, as a bonus, this also is how we can have both behaviors that are largely fixed as well as the experience of "free association".

Thus there seemingly is a meaningful analogy between the flow of energy across the natural streams of fluids (and development), and energy flowing laterally between neurons. Clearly, though, the matter is not this simple. Even so, we do unify divided flows back into unified objects and patterns with great facility, especially when these phenomena themselves have an internal causality cutting across the main flow (the wheat in the gust of wind). This does suggest that we may be integrating scenes such as these according to internal causalities that in some ways are *similar to* those that we sense must exist in unified phenomena. For we do understand such sights using a collection of one-dimensional action-potentials with which we perceive the very unity of forces underlying these scenes. In any event, this provides an analogy for a process that necessarily would differ significantly from fluid flows in the outside world, in spite of their causal similarities.

The likelihood is that inductional causal unities would have been an important original (evolutionarily) ability for the processing of object-detecting vision. Consider what would be needed for detecting fish or trilobites through the perceptions of the fluid movements of these marine animals. Cross-inductions could serve to unify the divided yet coordinated movements of these animals so that the observing animal could know it to be a single object. This unified "designation", or simply, perception, would also be integrating rationally with the perception of the rational forward movements of these animals as they are tracked against the contextual background[48].

Although there is significantly more to the binding question of consciousness than the foregoing considerations, being able to unify perceptions of the movements of both animals and of objects in the environment stands as a critical evolutionary imperative. Presumably the binding of these causally dependent movements mimics to some degree the causal unity in the natural object, yet because the lateral interactions between neurons has in all probability a nearly simultaneous effect across the entirety of one field made up of many fields, there are important differences. Worth mentioning as one of the greater differences is that the overall composition of the field affects each neuron as well as effecting itself through time as each neuron affects it. The overall field would appear to be

---

[48] Of course the Gestalt does not necessarily depend on such a process. The Gestalt, though, needs to occur on not just any sort of collection, and so it depends a great deal on habit, but in novel situations the hypothesis given here appears to be a reasonable way to perceive a unified organism.

the medium of causation (that is, beyond unconscious causation in action-potentials, of course), through which the information in the differences between neurons becomes effective as a causally changing energy form.

If incense smoke is, as it can be, considered as a collection of one-dimensional streams (ignoring diffusion) with a certain amount of cross-movement, the movement in the other dimensions acts causally primarily in a sequential fashion. However, in the nerves, the movement of action-potentials really is effectively one-dimensional through the nerve fibers, while there probably is a virtually instantaneous change in cross causation in the surrounding fields, and *in addition*, there is a sequential propagation of informed form laterally across the nerves, for the subdivisions of the field have stronger local effects than does the entire field. To be sure, even in a mechanical system such as the incense smoke, lateral propagation through the system can be quite rapid, but the quicker and finer (information-preserving) field effect unifies and binds our perception of incense smoke into an evolving convergent phenomenon as the sequential assimilation proceeds, while the actual smoke tends to diverge. The fact that lateral propagation takes place in a finite space in the brain also plays a large part in facilitating the unity that is so readily produced within the finely divided electro-magnetic field. As previously stated, convergence may also be facilitated by synapses filtering out the noise that tends to cause divergence, while order and convergence are promoted by the emergence of reinforcing signals (harmonics, etc.).

Causal intrusions into the interiors of nerve impulses

Whatever the overall effect of the forces cutting across the one dimension of the forward movement of the incense smoke, essentially the causality remains local there. The interesting question, though, is how these side forces would "feel" in the original one dimension in which the smoke (or more importantly, in the nerve-impulses modeling it) was traveling. In that single dimension its effect would be as an unknown force forward or backward—or both—coming out of nowhere to act on the single-dimensional flow. It would be kind of like the intrusion of the sphere in Flatland. Simple fluid flows would not, of course, be thought to be aware of such causal intrusions provoked by difference, yet within the nervous system, these intrusions of difference do seem to provoke consciousness, while sameness dulls awareness.

What we have are differences acting via induction on the one-dimensional flow in neurons from the outside. This is reminiscent of the so-called "internalization" of knowledge. And although that term as used is rather vague and seems to include processes *not* connected with induction, it is a useful concept for the essential process of incorporating the knowledge that exists not within firing neurons, but rather in the relations of a set, or sets, of firing neurons.

This returns the matter once more to causality, but on a somewhat different basis, and it brings the focus to an important feature of the conscious experience—the way in which we typically become conscious of things without objective continuity. Now there obviously is much continuity in consciousness, and we rely on these continuities. Nonetheless, thoughts come unbidden, and then simply "impress" themselves on our thought processes.

One might wonder why the inductive hypothesis would be at all superior to any other proposal for the cause of consciousness in explaining the mysterious appearance of conscious contents. After all, data simply must move from being not conscious (possibly the form is different in the unconscious data) to consciousness, given that we have nervous processes that are not conscious. And to be sure, if there are other reasonable hypotheses for the appearance of consciousness they might also provide a good explanation for the shift. Yet I would note here that if consciousness is riding on the causal forces of induction between neurons, the appearance of a conscious "entity" would be inevitable once a certain causal configuration of firings, thus of energy fields and their interactions, arose, for the form of the field itself would be an entity if we were observing it. This is to say that the induction concept of consciousness allows for nerve impulses to be or not to be conscious, given the properly enclosed, self-interacting sets of nerve impulses, and provides a real possibility for explaining conscious versus unconscious brain activity.

Induction would particularly involve the data of difference in its effect

What does seem to be the case is that the very sort of causal force that would act as an induction across differing energy fields around the neurons is the sort of which we experience consciously as detail, as difference. The greater the difference (provided it is somehow focal—literally focal in the case of vision), the greater the consciousness. Less difference, if it is reinforcing within certain parameters (harmonics, the moving fish), apparently boosts the overall level of consciousness, and may thus provide possibilities for contrast with the differences that do exist at the boundaries. Fortunately this should also work for phenomena not much considered in this book, and so perhaps a mass of color would create a self-reinforcing (conscious) signal as harmonics seem to do, only in this case the reinforcement would be due to proximity instead of to inductions across a distance.

A good aspect of the induction hypothesis for explaining consciousness is that it is not limited to either difference or sameness. Sameness seems to create an absolute signal, which, as mentioned above, quickly begins to dull the consciousness if it remains steady. This may make sense from an inductional standpoint, for perhaps as the differences which are causally effecting accelerations in the field of color as it is initially perceived in flux (that is, changing neuronal activity from what went on previously, and changing the context), consciousness of the color is aroused. Then, when the nerves have settled into a steady state, sort of a meta-equilibrium, so that inductional accelerations no longer occur to much of an extent, consciousness recedes. This would explain why some modern-day cartoons that are made with little movement in the scene (few frames per segment of time—cheap) are made more visually engaging by computer-generated fluctuations—especially in the outlines of the forms.

It may be that subtle experiments could be devised to empirically test the likelihood that the phenomenon of induction across nerves is the correlate of consciousness. If experimental data from competent testing did not support the thesis it would be disappointing, for it is an elegant solution to both the arousal and the fading of consciousness, based on nothing but the seemingly inevitable interactions of nerve-impulses in close proximity.

Importantly, experimental testing would have to check for the ability of the external force of fields (external from the "perspective" of the individual neuron) to induce an internal change within the affected nerve-impulse. Or probably more accurately, the internal force of the differentiated electro-magnetic field must be shown to create inductions in the action-potentials, as well as inductions having the proper data in them, in order for induction to appear to be strongly correlated with consciousness.[49] The differential embodied within the force field must eventually become incorporated into the flow of nerve-impulses, and this yields a somewhat different way of looking at consciousness—as the one-dimensional incorporation of the incidentals, the periphery, and the outside, into the ever-changing flux of consciousness.

The product of causal induction, the <u>tertium quid</u>, must be energy

One important question to ask if indeed 2-D differentials become a part of the 1-D flow of action-potentials (ignoring at present the opposite effect, for simplicity's sake) is, *what* do these become as they incorporate into the flow of nerve-impulses? Derrida would leave the differences as differences, letting the "trace" of which he writes absorb many of the problems and mysteries surrounding his ideas[50]. Nietzsche almost as unhelpfully calls the force driving the flux the will to power[51]. However, physics also has a mysterious "entity" which nonetheless serves us very well as a concept—energy. It has already been invoked as a "causal force" in this book. But an additional advantage of energy

---

[49] Keeping in mind that the "external" fields are not really separate from action-potentials, but can be causally considered in that way.

[50] Jacques Derrida's *Of Grammatology* is a good source for his ideas on the "trace"

[51] Nietzsche's *Beyond Good and Evil*, section 36, is a prime reference for this idea.

beyond the previously mentioned ones is that there is an absoluteness to the energy concept that makes it especially helpful in comprehending the absolute force of consciousness. For although many believe in free will, even these people are yet all too aware of the driving power of conscious thoughts. And if in fact the unconscious is the source of this, yet surely it is the "conscious force", the unconscious force as it becomes phenomenally conscious, that drives specific actions and the will.

One ought to remember that the binding problem is a constant issue surrounding mental processes. How the external and the abstract are able to bind internally with mental thoughts is one of the more important mind issues. Then there is the binding problem of consciousness *per se*, as well as the continuity across the gaps of harmonics. The so-called "assimilation", or as Hegel called it, "synthesis", is quite a real factor in our minds. It does appear that the binding force of in-formed energy acting within electro-magnetic fields, or the nerves that precisely shape actions, would have as absolute an effect as Hegel's absolutes, and not be causally underdetermined as in Derrida's scheme. For as we know from physics, the actualization of potential energy differences is fully determinate and precisely causal in its effect.

There is a strangeness to the abstract, to surfaces and what is seen, that philosophers continue to ponder. How is it that we are able to "assimilate" surface knowledge so that it becomes a part of the interior? While this is no place to discuss Hegel in any depth, the problem of the "syntheses" he proposed should be addressed by any hypothesis of consciousness. Hegel simply has no idea how it happens, except that it must be "absolute" in some cases. Could such a synthesis occur in the case of the information that is merely form and potential in a differential relation to two or more things? Energy can provide the medium for shifting such frustratingly relative data and potentials into actual and absolute phenomena within the brain, which explains how novel and "found" relationships can in reality become memory and "fact" within the brain. However, to do this requires that energy be actualized, and that it change from the potentials of Derridean differentials into absolute phenomena, such as nerve-impulses and the like.[52]

In this view, the preservation of causality is not a conscious creation, it is, rather, the becoming-conscious of thoughts, visualizations, etc., that produces consciousness. Thus consciousness, and consciousness of..., is really the same thing, in spite of the modifications that allow us to think of the two as different (a highly valuable feature that gives us the ability to project). One-dimensionality

---

[52] It should be mentioned here that ultimately I believe it is not primarily the actualization of information within neurons that correlates with consciousness, however useful the example is, and whatever the likelihood that it plays some role in consciousness.

of the nerves forces a becoming within the neurons as energy is laterally transferred. And the energies of the electro-magnetic field, or fields, are also in the flux of becoming.

The fluctual energy states in both of these are constrained by information (that is, by the magnitude and the configuration of the energy), and both are the register and account of what is becoming, within what is also passing-away. Hence the immense information accounted for by difference (what Derrida appreciated) is able to become known (or "known") by the nerve-impulses, the fields across the nerve-impulses, or both. And this is allowed by the simple expedient of the energy and information becoming a part of these media in such a comprehensive manner that the becoming amounts to a wide-scale integration of the informational context as well as providing for the becoming configurations of energies.

The breadth and the integrational tendencies of the inductional flux

The inherent advantage of induction for explaining the becoming of information, of consciousness, or more to the point, of both at once, is that it is a broadly-acting energy change in or across the neurons. The shifting magnitude and changing configuration occurring via induction is intrinsically integrational and subject to relatively fixed information such as we may receive from the unconscious, or the barest irreducible qualia out of the senses (color being such fixed data). It is an elegant explanation of consciousness because it accounts for the oddness of the conscious integration of what seems external—abstraction, surfaces, etc.—while agreeing with the constancy of perceptual data and the drives that so color and work beneath our conscious experience and "will".

Conservation of causal force was given as an earlier argument for a consciousness which exists as an account of information. But the same argument might apply to even digital and analog computers as well. We, however, are deeply involved in the becoming of consciousness, and of causality, yet it is again the routing of information from input to output that shows up the necessary workings of data and the interactions between data. Analog computers are in certain ways like the brain, with one huge difference. Analog computers produce an output that is to be observed—and the brain lacks an observer. In the brain, integration of data into output must be internalized into the stream of output— also the only opportunity for it to be known—and the driving differentials must cease to be mere potential. The potentials in the differentials have to produce an absolute configuration of data and energy for the correct efferent set of nerve-impulses to become a correct full-flowered entity which can create the properly formed and informed response within our complex environment. Our responses are, to repeat, also absolute. For there is nothing in us like in the computer, a reference (which is referenced to, of course, our own consciousness) against which to measure the force of the energy and the form of the data in the inflowing impulses and their differences.

This is to make the remark that the nature of our nervous output is such that external information held between nerve-firings has to become absolute output if it is to have the ability to direct our motor actions. The heart of information processing in the brain is in fact this delicate and necessarily information-conserving process—for there is nothing else with which to calibrate the constantly changing configurations of nerve-firings so as to make a response to it. Instead the externally-held differentials have to internalize, because the only output that matters is how the nerve firings are configured to provide one-dimensional impulses effectively to the motor organs.[53]

To proceed, the internal stream of each nerve is what triggers the target synapse or synapses, so that such information is fairly close to being digital (or "coded") in output as it is in the input. Meanwhile, the interactions in the brain happen according to differentials which have to be changed into something relatively digital. And it is these differentials that are primarily of what consciousness consists phenomenally, so that it is this need to re-arrange the energies of nerve-firings from the force of differentials which is highly suggestive of the notion that consciousness consists specifically in the process of this infusion (and loss) of force into precise energy/information arrangements. As in any "cause-effect" relationship, it is this kind of a correlation which suggests the causal relation, and there is no way to demonstrate that we could know beforehand that this "cause" would have "that effect"—part of the effect being consciousness. In other words, we could not know that causal induction might yield what we experience internally as consciousness, but if the two are simultaneously correlated, then this proposed causal relation has all of the evidence that can be required for causality.

The problem of becoming, consciousness, and induction

Although this is somewhat off the subject, one more consequence of this model of consciousness seems to be in its favor. Logically it appears that there should be no becoming. Parmenides made that point in his famous poem, and Zeno came up with a number of paradoxes to show the absurdity of motion and its relative, becoming. Some of these paradoxes do not look terribly convincing today, yet others, like the arrow paradox, indicate real problems with the

---

[53] No doubt there are interactions across nerves after leaving the brain, but presumably these are minimized, and set to happen according to fairly simple rules that leave the original configuration largely intact, if somewhat modified according to the specifics of the body.

reconciliation of motion, for example, with the logical structures against which we measure and perceive motion.

If, on the other hand, consciousness itself is a matter of becoming, via inductions into the interiors of our mind's information, and occurring in reference to relatively more stable data, it seems that our belief in the existence of stable information would almost necessarily coincide with the observation of becoming. Or again, in the case of the arrow, we observe the motion as it is becoming against the background of the rationalistic framework of vision. Paradoxically, it is indeed as Nietzsche proclaimed,[54] that insofar as observation shows us a becoming world, it does not lie, while our belief in stability is not supported by the senses. For we experience becoming—it is an empirical effect in consciousness—while the stable and rational knowledge we have has to be accepted as somehow "prior". And these assumptions often prove to be false (how that could happen is not our concern here).

One of the most intractable problems of both thought and consciousness (when the latter are treated separately as these often are—erroneously) has been how there can be the incorporation of the non-integral differential data into the stream of consciousness, informing the output. This is because it has typically been considered a computing problem—in fact, often considered a little problem because the brain tends to be thought of as a computer (a reason for the problem remaining intractable)—however there is no sum yielding a product in the brain as there is in a digital computer. And the long chain of cause and effect of the analog computer is unlike the brain. Instead, the brain incorporates the differentials as absolute changes in the magnitude and configuration of the divisions of its energies, subtly shifting the sets of nerve-impulses in a process that seems clearly to coincide with the consciousness of differential details within the total context. Thus the induced becoming stands as the non-rational conscious record of the associational process which allows us to recognize the rational referents against which becoming is observed. In other words, becoming provides the relative motion which allows us to recognize stable structures of logic—and even of the world.

Whether or not it solves the problem, this apparently is what actually happens.

---

[54] Nietzsche, *Twilight of the Idols*, "'Reason' in Philosophy" section 2.

Chapter 7:

Activating potentials to fluidize information

Derrida, Jung, and their different differentials

De Saussure set the stage for Derrida to develop a linguistic theory of sheer difference in which word differentials drive each other forward in an essentially Newtonian mechanism of cause and effect, if not with the strict determinism of Newtonianism. It has its value, especially as a counter to the earlier logocentric philosophies with their dualistic tendencies. Nietzsche had already called into question the dualism that predominates from Plato on down to Hegel. Dualisms even pervaded the teachings of the pre-Socratic philosopher of the flux, Heraclitus. Nietzsche, however declined to set up his own encompassing theory to oppose to dualism—in other words, he did not fall for the dualistic trap of Derrida (who denies that he has himself). So it remained to Derrida to make an important and useful theory, cut off from much of the psychology of language, that could reveal the pure possibilities of one of the processes driving the actions of language.

However, the attraction and force of dualism should not be forgotten as easily as Derrida seems to have—and which, to his credit, Nietzsche did not. Jung, on the other hand, pushes Freudian dualisms (thought to be partly derived from Hegel) to a very prominent position in his psychology, quite possibly too far in the direction opposite Derrida. To whatever extent Jungian psychology deserves criticism, though, it is a very colorful, powerful world of deep oppositions, leading to the resolutions of opposition—the magical symbols of transformation. To a considerable degree Jung simply treads a familiar Heraclitean path, not so much explaining what is going on, but documenting a flux of interpretation surrounding oppositions and their resolutions, caught up in the Grimm world of magical transformations. However that may be, Jung seems to leave little doubt that oppositions really do play a large role in depth psychology, and that these produce a powerful symbolism of transformation.

A problem arises when trying to fit the generally large magnitude dualities of Jung and his antecedents into the becoming of nerve inductions. These oppositions almost certainly are on a scale greater than the inductions across neurons, and perhaps greater even than the typical inductions across differing sets of neurons that under this book's hypothesis are proposed to occur. One cannot be certain that the oppositions of good and evil, male and female, or up and down, are merely larger scaling of the gap in the differentials of words, thoughts, or variations in the perceptions we have of the rippling of a glinting fish or field of wheat. For it could be that the presumed neural correlates of the oppositions differ significantly from the cross-inductions of neurons or of sets of neurons. Yet consciousness of these oppositions and the symbols that unite them seems no different from the other differentials, except in magnitude. And even if the "oppositions" are not simply based on differentials, surely a real possibility is that the oppositions at least provide an analogy for the resultants of the smaller differentials, perhaps lending insight into the effects of both dualities and the other conscious content.

Oppositions apparently have powerful conscious effects

Awareness—consciousness—of difference seems to come about most easily in the case of oppositions. The familiar problem of the lack of prior references is, or so one might conjecture, solved in the case of oppositions by what it produces, a large energy effect which often manifests itself in part by the so-called symbols of transformation. It is not clear exactly what something like the good-evil opposition produces. Perhaps its correlates are primarily feelings of hatred, disgust, fear, and the like, but whatever its result, the effect of good vs. evil on consciousness seems to be great[55]. Certainly the symbols of transformation of good and evil, such as Jesus on the cross, are powerful. Like the male-female oppositions that tend to be ever-present in the more primitive societies, it is true that the common good-evil distinction is complex, with resolutions to be found in a complex of symbols, actions, and rituals.

Notwithstanding the complexity of the oppositions, the crucial role of oppositions for valuing seems incontrovertible whether these are extremes of the visual field, the powers of sexuality and its male-female dichotomy, or perhaps the most important of all, the judgments of good and bad, or good and evil. There is no reason to repeat here the many examples and considerations given to the oppositions by Jung. What is most important now is that stretching between the opposites, especially if these neutralize each other, is the symbol or act.

Sexual union is the great act and symbol of the clash and resolution of the two sexes, yet it must be remembered that a great many symbols (the child being one of the most obvious and common ones) also represent the difference, separateness, and also the union of the opposing forces of male and female. Lest it should be argued that sexual dualism is an inevitable outcome of the evolution of sexual creature, thus not lending itself to extension to the rest of the world, it must be replied simply that not only dualism, but especially sexual dualism, plays

---

[55] Actually, this is not to claim that the good-evil opposition is primary at all, and apparently a number of oppositions are collected under that Manichean dualism of good/evil. But surely this is not done for no cause (if that is what happens), but because the various oppositions are experienced as absolute contraries, and this is the effect that accounts for good and evil being in the discussion here.

a very important role in the primitive understanding of the world. For instance, alchemy is full of sexual symbolism, as Jung has shown. Creation myths—thus ancient cosmologies—are full of sexual dualism and union, with Semitic myth and Hesiod's *Theogony* providing a small sample of a very widespread phenomenon. And the genders commonly seen in languages such as French and Latin, not to mention the past dual numbers of nouns and verbs in Greek, all seem to show important influences on earlier beliefs about the greater world from the extremely important "opposition" of the sexes.

The other symbols of dualities, their forces, and often their resolutions, are created things, like the earth, sacrifices, rituals, and intermediates of all kinds. The Grimm tales are full of magical objects that are related to resolutions of the clash of opposites—flowers, magical roots (the latter being in Homer, too), and any number of exquisite prizes of ordeals (the golden bird, etc.). Things appear from the massive potentials created by the encounter of opposites, yet a significant aspect links these Jungian oppositions to the phenomena on which Derrida concentrated. This is the underdetermined[56] nature of phenomena in our consciousness—which is especially noticeable in language. For the symbols of opposition, unless ritualistically or narratively fixed (or in some less familiar way), are typically numinous, changeable, and not due to simple causal chains but instead to difficult-to-predict conjunctions of unlike forces.

The crux of this for the inductional explanation of opposites and their effects, is that there is apparently a power created when the opposites meet. The more fundamental the opposites, the less determined the resultant force appears to be, possibly because the fundamental drives are themselves not very precise (even if they may be relentlessly goal-oriented), but driving to something yet to be determined[57]. Now it should be added that there is no reason to believe that "opposites" as we consider them are necessarily oppositional in terms of the nerve-firings themselves, and these could in fact even be complementary[58] in producing a resultant force and effect. The only point crucial here is that, as it is with smaller differentials (which I consider simply to create differential effects

---

[56] Underdetermined according to what we know prior to our consciousness of the matter is what I mean here, not at all a fundamental underdetermination. On the fundamental level, underdetermination is what I believe is exactly what consciousness prevents, through its very strong deterministic aspect.

[57] To assert that the fundamental drives are not precise or determined is meant to be taken relative to the phenomenal aspect of our minds, and not as implying that they are not definite physically.

[58] However it would seem that if complementary, the nerve-firings would have, in some way, to be incompatible, at least partially. Perhaps this would be due to certain "codes" or the result of being upper or lower harmonics which oppose in number but agree energetically.

through induction), these greater "opposite" differentials seem to produce a sizeable resultant force. This *seems* to be roughly proportional in power with the greater potential that produced them, as experienced according to our perceptions of their differences (there may be problems of circularity in such perceptions and experiences, but in its depth, thinking about the mind regularly runs into such problems, and we simply have to try to deal with them).

Hence the issue here is merely opposites as we know these to be phenomenally so, since it is true that in a very real sense we only know them as their difference—we know the force of their difference. Furthermore, whether the so-called opposites reacted inductively as somehow "plus" and "minus" (thus, as electrical fields or opposite magnetic poles), or instead, as competitive "opposites" constructively reinforcing nerve-impulses, the resulting force of energy might be the same in either case provided that the magnitudes were equal. As long as the product of induction is relatively indeterminate or underdetermined (vis-à-vis desired human goals, that is), a powerful force is created which searches for actions and symbols of actions. These opposites provide the most powerful sorts of example of how presumable difference can generate the force for the conscious existence of mental objects, around which actions are either perceived, or held in the imagination for the purpose of possible action.

The *tertium quid* of energy coming out of the clash of opposites[59]

As somewhat of an example, it should be noticed that physics has reached into the imagination of the opposites for a number of its concepts. Plus and minus, and oppositions analogous to the magnetic poles, have already been mentioned, but these concepts of opposites also go well beyond the electromagnetic force—even the strong nuclear force can shift sign. Although it is true in physics these concepts are subsumed more generally under the broader principle of symmetry, this does not obviate oppositions of forces, rather more confirming the concept. The matter-antimatter distinction, and what happens as a consequence of contact between matter and its opposite, is understood according to opposition. What is more, the fact of matter-antimatter collision appears to be as true as anything we know about the outside world.

Like the possibilities for "opposition" in the mind, one could consider the energy that comes out of matter-antimatter annihilation as representing the magnitude of difference between matter and antimatter ("equal and opposite"

---

[59] I am, of course, aware that many physicists would not think of energy as being different from mass. But for us this does not matter—phenomenally energy is different from particles, and this goes equally for mental objects and the "physical objects" which we also happen to know through mental objects.

particles). Or one could get the same results by a model in which "masses" are added complementarily to produce the energy according to the equation $E=mc^2$. Either way, it would seem likely that our best bet for understanding the way in which we view matter-antimatter collision would be according to events similar in many respects to it (as these come out of our means of understanding). Therefore it would tentatively follow from this argument that the concepts of the resultants of oppositions in our brains happen according to the difference between opposites, or through the addition of similar opposing energies, with little to distinguish the two ideas. For the result of bringing two relatively definite objects together[60] in opposition is an undefined (that is, according to the original parameters) and fluid energy, which only later becomes defined in relation to something else.

The process of relating information is essential—it could be quantum

The matter anti-matter collision, of course, gives us an analogy of the brain and the energies within it to a quantum phenomenon, annihilation and the subsequent definition of the resulting energy after the destruction of the particle-antiparticle pair. Apparently the possibility broached by Penrose[61] and others, that quantum processes may explain the mind, deserves some consideration, even though I believe that the interface of any possible quantum brain states with the non-quantum world is a more important issue.

For myself, the most plausible candidate for a quantum procedure in the mind would come as a result of inductions across sets of nerve-firings that produce "new" energies not defined by former phenomena. These might eventually become defined according to the surrounding energies and particles, but especially the energies (in fields), which may not be as susceptible to thermal decoherence as atoms and molecules. In addition, inductions of energy may result in something like the phonons in crystals which may initially be relatively undefined, then come slowly into an "awareness" of context and neighboring particles.

On the other hand, I do not believe that it especially matters, and that quantum entanglement of a hypothetical particle coming out of induction serves primarily as a good example of the fluid movement of information between the induced energy and the contextual energy surrounding it which seems to describe our experience[62]. Essentially the whole question comes down, again, to the issue

---

[60] These objects could be particle-antiparticle or "opposed" sets of nerve firings.

[61] Penrose's *The Emperor's New Mind* is a prime source for quantum ideas about consciousness.

[62] Perhaps entanglement with the thermal motions of the brain is not immediate as long as the energy in fields (maybe, but less likely, in nerve-impulses) is not strictly tied to

of **becoming** when an induction occurs, something that appears to correlate well with our internal experience of consciousness. Whether this becoming has quantum aspects, a reasonable proposal, or if it merely exists according to what would have to occur in any sort of electrical or magnetic induction when considered apart from quantum mechanics, the coordinated shifting of information in a fluid context of energy and information is the crucial aspect of the becoming of the induction, though perhaps quantum effects would make the process more fluid[63]. The information involved is driven on through internal energy changes, and we maintain an account of these changes through the interior of our consciousness. Thus we become aware of the thought even as it is forming in accordance with association (induction being the obvious explanation of association), while it is fluid and causal. As becoming—change—starts to disappear, so, too, does the consciousness of the thought.

Whether quantum or otherwise, the becoming of an induction happens in accordance with the internality of the information of the system in which the induction occurs. Crucially, only the interior of the becoming can "know" the reciprocally interacting energies and information that dictates how the induction and the energy and information themselves develop. And it is this that constitutes our conscious experience.

---

particles. This would be a quantum reason for my preference that consciousness be described as, primarily at least, according to the more independent electrical and magnetic fields around the nerves than in the action-potentials driven by the movement of ions.

[63] I will reiterate here the important fact of nervous systems from *Hydra* to us—energies within the system must be distributed and shaped until the proper output is created. Induction would be a prime candidate for this, especially since it conserves information and energy, and the induction would have to accord and conform with the changing energy and information of the nerve in which it is induced.

Chapter 8:

Information interacting in fields is the best analogy with consciousness

"Freedom" in a will incorporating potentials

Oddly, and not in agreement with my intention, last chapter ended with the possibility that some resultants from dualistic oppositions could be actually undefined, if certain quantum functions occur as a part of induction. However, that, along with a certain sort of free will, is tolerable in an explanation of human thinking and behavior as long as the precipitating factors (emotions and drives especially) are substantially controlled by nature and nurture, and the force of our drives is informed by the very great amount of information coursing through differentials and the nerves. After all, it must be understood that the best argument against the quantum conceptions of consciousness of someone like Penrose is that we are not at all as free and unpredictable as his model would make us out to be. Neither psychology nor sociology will allow a will anywhere near as free as most theorists of quantum consciousness make the will out to be.

Surely there must be some sense, though, in giving allowance for what we seem to experience—free will. After all, probably the best argument for "free will" is that we do get to decide what we are going to do, as evidenced by the struggle with which we make said decision. Within the present hypothesis of consciousness, the argument principle against the perception of free will would be that consciousness actually occurs within and is heavily in-formed by, a context of information. Yet if a deterministically causal force were to produce a thought, deterministically yet eventually de-linking from causal data, the thought could be sensed as "free" when it has simply lost context. Strangely enough, however, even a version of this may also allow a sort of free will. This is because a quantity of energy produced by its informational and energetic becoming may very much be a potential ready to be defined by the specific information in the finely-divided energy fields and nervous impulses coming from perception and memory (among other sources). That is to say, turning the direction of the last sentence around, a potential that is causally determined can energize other information even while its own data lack any more meaning than noise. Within the sense of *meaning* it could be free though determined.

In any case, whether the "will" be free or unfree, the interesting condition of it is that while the energies of the drives as well as the oppositions are both very powerful and ill-defined by meaning, the symbols of transformation (typically between opposites) appear to exist *as the power of* the energies resulting from the oppositions and the drives. Meanwhile the form is derived from a wide variety of data driven in accordance with their differences and magnitudes of their energies. This is not, surely, to say that the energies coming out of the deep psyche do not drive the data as well, for indeed these forces can energize the more peripheral data, to make what has become dull and lifeless, alive and meaningful—and not incidentally, significantly more conscious.

However, it does appear that, despite the hierarchical predominance of the more powerful psychic forces in many cases, these tend to become in-formed, informed, by the data which are definite, and thus to "take up" or "take in" this information "of its own accord", so to speak. The reciprocal nature of the interactions of the two different sets of nerve impulses allows, again, for an "identity" to occur between the nervous force coming out of the brain's potential and the force of the incoming data. And, of course, inductions provide one of the best candidates for these reciprocal interactions.

The force to "program" nerve responses

What is vital at this point is that dualities at least can be an analogy for inductional difference on the lower scale, apparently producing what would be expected from induction, a force and energy which can exist iconically in the mind as a symbol. But if, on the other hand, the actions and symbols coming out of the clash of difference—or simply out of a more or less single psychic force—were set and predictable, our actions might then be evidences of the relatively fixed response one should expect of the slowly changing nerves and synapses of the brain. In fact, it seems that there could be little to re-program the brain if nerves and synapses did all or nearly all of the processing. For a synaptic summary flattening could readily come out of an adaptive brain consisting in just nerves and synapses, but how could intricate coordinated responses be imposed onto synaptic probabilities? In other words, how could nerves and synapses produce our precise coordinated actions through their own imprecision and probabilities?

The reality is that for there to be much of a coordinated fluidity to "program" the adaptable synapses of the brain requires a precision and preservation of knowledge far beyond that of ordinary synapses, and especially beyond the adaptable synapses. To put it another way, something other than the probabilistic synapses has to both hone habitual responses and (probably) to coordinate even these each time. Happily enough, we seem to know this fluid force well internally, as consciousness. "Externally" it appears to be representable through the familiar, if still somewhat mysterious, induction seen in electro-magnetism.

Fortunately, induction along with the more set activities of action-potentials in nerves allows for feedback in the "programming" of nerves. Interacting fields can shape nerve responses, and then once the action is performed, perceptual data serve to correct the deviations from what was desired. Thus nerves and synapses are honed by perception, not only of original sensory data, but also by perception of the actions produced by nerves. There is indeed a "force" behind the successes of nerves, and it is one that can shape and adapt nerve impulses.

Although we evidently can sense the depth of many drives and emotions, they still seem to be known, at least for the most part, where difference arises. That is, consciousness of the drives and emotions comes about either in clashes with each other[64] or at details and perceptions. The coordination and complexity that arise here, however, are what bring Nietzsche, and especially Derrida, to question the dualistic world—however, fortunately for a Nietzschean like myself, Nietzsche does not insist on it. The power of difference is shown most intensely in the dualisms, while the result of these seem to be formed according to shifting forces and causations—to be almost quixotically shaped by the moment.

For this reason, although I have generally focused on the problem of moving energy, and thus information, across nerves to create the needed set of action-potentials for action, consciousness itself looks as though it most probably exists chiefly in the forces surrounding, and therefore directing, the nerve impulses. On the most cursory level we do seem to go through the trouble of directing what will happen, and the interactions of the fields around nerves could very well afford us the vantage point from which this can occur. I do not know why the need for this second and different form of mental processing has generally not occurred to people, other than believers in the soul, but perhaps it is simply because there was no obvious answer to the problem.

Conscious fields versus unconscious forces in the nerves

The usefulness of the induction idea for explaining associations has already been covered. Here it should be clearly pointed out that field interactions and nerve inductions may well be separated conceptually and that one appears preferable as an explanation for conscious cognition. Accounting for consciousness should work better if the primary part of the conscious direction of brain activity were in the electro-magnetic fields themselves, instead of in the many individual neuronal inductions, for obviously a wide variety of data are interacting at one time in association. It does appear, in the case of the symbols of the unconscious, that field interactions explain why the conscious forms of these symbols to appear to be as fluid as they do, their *forms* unconstrained by the considerable power of the emotions and drives. Unconscious drives and activations by the oppositions need to have fluid responses, in order that these responses may be shaped and formed by our perceptions of our environment.

---

[64]This could be why we are prone to dualistic thought—because once two mental forces clash, these become conscious, tending to prevent another from coming in, unless it is danger or something else that drives out the other two.

Importantly, while consciousness does tend to follow the aims to which the drives and emotions are directing, no direct ties between consciousness and the drives are necessary, perhaps not even possible. The so-called states of repression and sublimation are unnecessary hypotheses, since the drives and emotions are simply providing for action, which if all goes well, satisfies whatever triggered the drives and emotions. If the need behind the drives and emotions is not satisfied, of course, the problem continues and "repression" can definitely be diagnosed. But that diagnosis is a fiction based, presumably, on the simple fact that so far the actions produced by the drive have not satisfied the end for which the drive arose, and to which it tended to direct. It is the consciousness that has to direct and combine the flow of nerve impulses from the drive and from the perceptions in order to deal with the human's environment, for the power of the "unconscious" requires heavy interpretation in our inconstant world.

This "dual" processing of conscious and unconscious allows both to operate and insist on their priority within each of their realms without any especial conflict. The emotions and drives need not be conscious at all, yet are insistent and persistent, directing ends that people do not realize they have. One may presume that drives and emotions tend to originate and exist primarily as nerve firings, and thus to be unconscious until some sort of differential is produced with an "opposing" or conflicting drive or emotion. Or differentials may simply be produced in inductive association with conscious perceptions, thus bringing emotions and drives to phenomenal experience. So thus consciousness of emotions and drives appear to be explainable as secondarily derived, while the primary force of drives and emotions would in such a scenario exist apart from consciousness *per se*, in considerable force of the nerve firings themselves. Consciousness remains in this scenario free to act on the emotions and drives, and even sometimes contrarily to at least some of them. It therefore can process information and shift the energy-information complex to useful ends.

The above is written to indicate the sort of explanatory value of inductional consciousness vis-à-vis what we know or suspect concerning the conscious and the unconscious. What it does not do is to explain the physical reason for why it is that consciousness apparently correlates better with the shift in the subdivided electro-magnetic fields than with the shift from these fields and the nervous firings themselves. I have used resonances as a primary example to demonstrate why induction looks to be necessary. This seemed an acceptable example because it entails interaction of the fields from the way such a phenomenon would apparently have to occur. And when induction moves to more detailed information, whether it is the energy transfer between fields and from fields into action-potentials the same information is essentially involved, hence to demonstrate the explanatory value of induction for consciousness could as easily correlate consciousness with the field interactions, with the inductions *per se*, or with both.

For this very reason it is difficult to separate the two conceptually, particularly as they are not truly separate physically. Electro-magnetic fields interact continuously with the electrical (plus chemical in the case of nerves) phenomena which are embedded in them, and which are often thought of as giving rise to the fields (in fact they are probably better thought of as mutually causal once established). Nevertheless, as previously noted, the fields are acting somewhat separately from nerves, and provide for data interactions which can direct the other forms of data interaction, as consciousness evidently does.

So it is in some ways moot and hardly crucial to the induction-consciousness hypothesis to know whether the fields or inductions are more conscious. There still is reason to ask which "part" of the nerve-firings is more conscious. And this reason is, at its simplest, in order to argue for the subdivided electro-magnetic fields of the brain as the director conscious activity, and thus of the efferent nervous output.

Honing nerve signals through non-nerve information processing

One of the reasons to think that consciousness mostly skates along the fields and the energy-information transfers associated with them, is the previously mentioned matter of our experience being one of conscious honing of our activities. Indeed this seems to be a predominant activity of consciousness. Consider how Achilles remains focused on Hector as he aims at him. Simply by consciously concentrating, his well-honed nerves come closer and closer to an output that can result in a hit just where he wishes. Or, as I write, my consciousness as I experience it is of having possibilities which are not yet fully concretized for the action of typing, but will be if I let my (mental) perceptions continually direct my actions. Now it is true that these are merely suggestive of field interactions that are quicker than the induction into nerves[65]. There are hugely complex sets of nerve-firings, feedback, and I would propose some fairly free "endless loops" in parallel, all of which no doubt have more capabilities than we have ever discovered. However, this honing experience of ours does appear to agree with the idea of field interactions (hence, of consciousness) outstripping the speed of nervous induction.

---

[65] Facilitating this view is that induction of nerve-firings cannot be as simple or nearly as quick as induction in a copper wire, because action-potentials occur according to relatively fixed electrical and chemical parameters, while field interactions are much more free and speedy, thus paradoxically allowing information interactions and complexity to a degree not otherwise possible.

Too much information interacts at once to happen in separate nerves

The second reason to prefer the primacy of field interactions as the correlate of consciousness is also not new. It is that a wide range of information evidently interacts in a continual complex evolution within the consciousness. The context of whatever it is upon which we are focusing is now well known from cognitive studies to color our response to whatever "entity" we are sensing[66]. And again the fact can be brought up that, while the entirety of interactions in the brain is too complex to pretend it can truly be characterized, the seamless interaction of so much information at once would fit the field-interaction as correlate of consciousness the best. The fluid interactions of dreams and dream-like states supports the field-interaction hypothesis even better, it should be recognized— and this is precisely when some of the constraints of visual processing which provides us with a stable picture is missing. Apparently, the more the visual field is merely conscious (as I believe is the case in dreams—and if not, in the psychedelic experience) and the less it is processed, the more it shifts to state existing in a fluidly associational manner which is poorly remembered.[67]

One could hearken back to the hypothesized resonance inductions, as well, to support the field-interaction predominance in consciousness. To repeat an earlier concept, we have very good memory of much music, and poor memory of resonance (we may re-create some of the resonance that we do hear when our minds "play it back"), again suggesting that resonance as conscious supports a certain firing of nerves that represents notes, while permitting the conscious detail to finally disappear. The rich and precise information interactions of consciousness allows us to remember notes accurately from the resultant, and preserved, firings, while there is not nearly enough nerve capacity, let alone memory capacity, to represent the information content of consciousness.

There is a way around the dominance of field-interaction as consciousness-correlate, it being one of the reasons I did not earlier distinguish between it and induction in the nerves. As it happens, electric and magnetic fields are set up by the action-potentials initiated by the synapses. Of course, the fields themselves are induced by the nerve firings, and then the two do so reciprocally. One could easily have consciousness exist from a complex interaction of inductions between fields and nerves, nerves and fields, and between fields and fields, making an

---

[66] To just mention one example, Edwin Land's retinex theory of color perceptions notes the importance of the contextual fact of the light illuminating a scene.

[67] The issue of memory is important, since memory is presumably caused by formed sets of action-potentials which partially re-create a similar conscious mental object when retrieved (with a lot of detail lost). Dream-states with free-association may be poorly remembered precisely because so much of it is not fixed into nerve firings (because not finalized into finite actions), rather shifting around for certain types of association.

overall unity (unity is essential to explain consciousness) without an overall field. And I would in fact suspect that some of each does play some part in consciousness. However, as stated previously, the speed and fluidity of consciousness, and especially the manner in which data seem to interact simultaneously rather than serially, appears to correlate significantly better with data transfer across fields instead of through the slow inductions that probably occur among fields and action-potentials.

We learn data that exist at the periphery of our drives and desires

A third and more difficult to argue for field-interactions as the prime correlate of consciousness is the suspicion I have that much of our best learning comes naturally and peripherally. This relates to Gestalts and induction, of course, but has considerable aspects of its own. The point being that when we are conscious of an entirety, the parts naturally integrate into the "whole" which is our perception, yet we often realize later that we "learned" of an important relationship. People who progress intellectually evidently pick this up, and are not especially cognizant of the details even though they can be aware of them if called to do so. These details so-called do not, naturally, include the extreme amount of information contained in consciousness, but they do include nonetheless fairly complex relationships seamlessly integrated (via even greater conscious complexity which is lost as it becomes unconscious) into rather matter-of-fact memories.

Information spins into the memories and pictures we retain, that is. Presumably we do not truly remember the relationships inherent in remembered scenes that we later extract, but in recalling the pictures we can replay some of the conscious interactions and use these (with other conscious additions) to direct an analysis of the interactions if we wish. This could be because we re-integrate the picture, and in the doing we reproduce some of the less data-rich but more select (and probably somewhat artificial) information originally integrated into it. Thus, by making memories conscious again we are able to interpret the picture and extract the data that were spun into it. And this, too, seems to indicate a relatively widespread interaction such as could occur across a subdivided electro-magnetic field, without having to revert the data back to nerves in the process.

I repeat that this is a difficult argument and far from conclusive, yet I bring it in because of the importance of learning the peripheral knowledge that we do. It is common, but little remarked, and this strikes me as strange because so much of this largely rational knowledge is so typically not the focus of vision or of attention, and yet it is so thoroughly integrated into the picture. Since we do not seem to have to think about it, merely letting it into our consciousness, the processing would apparently happen quite naturally and reasonably quickly within our conscious minds. Induction is the easy, accurate, and precise means of creating a high-value data-rich picture, and it could likewise quickly spread the information of a novelty, or of a recognized danger, throughout consciousness (and the latter is especially quick), thus allowing attention to be focused on it (and thus sensory data sought).

The main point about the peripheral data we pick up, though, is that it is processed, but not by conscious exertion if it is not remarkable. Instead it seems merely to be an aspect of consciousness, like the integration of the wheat field in the wind, and it is not stored as a knowledge of such an integration, but merely as an integrated picture. Like the many conscious details that are lost to memory, so is the conscious processing of many of even the larger details, which appears to indicate that these data do not fully become a part of the set of action-potentials that create a memory, but rather shape the data that *are* preserved in memory. And since the same inductional hypothesis also seems to allow for the quick movement of danger signals throughout consciousness by disrupting even the context of one's focus (for example, peripheral vision), it has explanatory value.

The becoming of the conscious flux

The last reason for field-interactions to be what we experience as consciousness is that it best agrees with the continuous becoming of the conscious flux and of conscious objects. Because of the continuity of nervous impulses with the fields around them, this does not by itself exclude nerve induction from consciousness. I would be loathe to suggest this exclusion at any rate, but were nerve induction *per se* to play too great a role there would be a tendency for information to drop out of the conscious mix too easily. To be sure, energy and information are continually falling out of the field, and new energy and information coming into it, but each moment of consciousness, and each conscious object or conscious flow has a continuity with itself until it presumably disappears into relatively non-interacting sets of nerve impulses that make up the unconscious.

This last reason for preferring consciousness' residence in field interactions is a good deal like the first reason, but this one is insisting on the coherence of consciousness (with its neural correlate), and its ability to create effects without an excessive loss of some portions of data to nerves during conscious coherence. In fact this argument is deliberately repeating the necessity of comprehensive data processing within consciousness, which would seem necessarily to exist as a somewhat separate force for the purpose of directing action-potentials. Symbols of transformation and other Gestalts have to form the nerve impulses internally, across the information-rich "boundaries" connecting the divisions of the electro-magnetic fields, which is to note that first the overall information internalizes into the overall field. The informational fields have to be made and in-formed prior to their direction of, and therefore their incorporation into, the nerve signals.

And like induction in the nerves, this involves energy inputs that have significant information in them, so then both the original information/energy complex and that of the new influx have to come into relation in this other form of a becoming. Information relationships can presumably be much more complex and rich than the actual inductions in the nerves. This does not really preclude consciousness occurring mostly in the nerve inductions, however, but this is a simpler and more direct correlation of the comprehensive nature of consciousness with the comprehensive nature of a large, if subdivided, electro-magnetic field existing across sets of nerves. More importantly, it seems a better account of the way in which we make judgments of "identity" when they are not actually identical, for an information-absorbing field is what can best hold onto a sort of inclusive informational identity even while it shifts and changes.

Nerves and synapses provide the stability against which the fields may interact

Nerve impulses and the inductive changes of these impulses are crucial, however, to the energy interactions in the fields associated with them. It is the action-potentials that resist energy/information changes, thus preventing the nerves from simply collectively adding all of the brain's information into a single nervous output. Instead it has to be shared in a "broadband" so to speak, and the information in the fields must develop itself according to itself. This is how we can process information (in conjunction with the procedures and summations of synapses), thereby shifting sets of nerve firings, and thus creating models of reality that may be useful in the future.

As Derrida correctly points out, the words in a text are seriously underdetermined, even in its literary context. Yet we do not read Homer merely for anthropology. There is a serious and highly complex interaction of the underdetermined words, the human context of experience, and the underdetermined rhythms and sequences of the text that make it extremely rich, if admittedly never quite reproducing itself in the way it was. And it was in poetry like that of Homer's that complex information was able to be transferred most efficiently from human to human when literacy was non-existent to scarce. For the complex interactions of words, meanings, rhythms and the like creates a sequential symbolization[68], indeed a flux, and thus represent the product of a repeatable (if not *exactly* repeatable) mental process which can extract more information than is stored by the mere words themselves, via the substantial *human* context.

---

[68] I do not intend to even begin to broach, in this work (or probably ever), temporal memory, such as is in music and poetry.

That is to say that conscious analysis can figure out what conscious synthesis never noticed, as the latter consciousness is the result of some fairly automatic data processing regardless of the novelty of the information. Again it is worth noting that the accuracy of these symbols, or memorized Homeric verse, could not happen via synapses but rather through complex, interacting fields, or the like. Quantum consciousness proponents are right about one thing at the very least—nerves and synapses are not by themselves adequate to explain what we know and think.

Finally, then, I should state that consciousness as the correlate of interactions between the fine divisions of the brain's electro-magnetic fields is my preference because of the sheer immensity of information interaction possible in this phenomenon. Energy transfers, with their concomitant information transfers, are what could cause consciousness, because the enormous information content shifts according to shifting (and often novel) information that we know to exist in consciousness, and this seems possible only within the massive intersection of many small, high-data, fields.

Chapter 9:

The non-universal mind—consciousness as a momentary flux

Getting away from the temptation of pan-psychism

Naturally, the "problem" of pan-psychism arises as a question when consciousness is viewed according to interacting fields, induction, or both, for why should other electro-magnetic phenomena not therefore be conscious? David Chalmers is one of the prominent advocates of pan-psychism, and interestingly enough he brings up the old idea of consciousness being somehow the ripple in an electrical field that was fairly common in the early 1900's, and mentioned favorably by Bertrand Russell[69]. However, the ideas presented in this book differ significantly from any version of the earlier electrical field theory of consciousness.[70] Likewise, I was not dependent upon these ideas for my own. My own track proceeded to induction and field interactions from the desire to find a way to move peripheral and boundary information into thoughts, models, and (mental) objects. I believe that pan-psychism can be avoided because of the low or non-existent consciousness in so many brain activities, and because it seems that there is a plausible way, induction, of moving boundary information into the nerves, the field of consciousness.

After this introduction I need also to point out that I do not understand the animus many have against pan-psychism. We really do not know that anything at all may not be conscious in its internal existence, in its dynamic. Even the obvious difficulty of not being able to test what Chalmers claims is no worse than the problem of not having a means to test the unconsciousness of, for instance, telephone networks. This does not void the question of whether or not Chalmers has really said anything beyond obvious possibilities, but at least there is little reason to conclude *a priori* that pan-psychism either cannot or should not be.

I make this statement about pan-psychism in part because I do not believe that it can be ruled out, and some very bare "awareness" in electro-magnetic phenomena may in fact be what underlies our consciousness. Yet I have to admit that I would not prefer a conscious inanimate world, nor do I recognize much evidence that it is, for we seem not to form much of any mind-meld with the

---

[69] See David Chalmers. *The Conscious Mind.* New York: Oxford University Press, 1996. pp. 134-136. And see Bertrand Russell. *The Analysis of Matter.* New York: Dover Publications, Inc., 1954. p. 320.

[70] At least it appears different than the several authors I read after coming up with my own, hoping that I was not merely duplicating earlier ideas.

various foreign objects that sometimes lodge in brains. On the contrary, foreign objects, including electrical things, appear best able to destroy portions of brain processes such as consciousness. Furthermore, considerable brain processing seems to occur without consciousness being involved within these particular processes at all. While the possibility cannot be ruled out that nerve processes controlling the body may have their own consciousnesses without these linking up with the rest of our conscious mind, it would appear to be difficult to keep these two consciousnesses separate, especially without exception.[71] A holistic, complex, and indeed somewhat fragile, cause of consciousness stands as the best candidate to explain a state that is evidently rather limited in scope even within our central nervous systems.

Stability of information and categories in consciousness, versus in electricity

One of the reasons, in fact, to consider induction to correlate with the internal causation of consciousness is that mental phenomena simply appear in consciousness, then are immediately interacting with differing sorts of data from disparate sources. These different sorts of data do not simply mingle and lose their characters, rather they subtly (if not *always* subtly) change each other—exchanging data without loss of the qualities of data that these are (at least seemingly not while conscious). So it appears that Nietzsche was right to identify the flux as an overwhelming feature in our conscious minds, but he seemed to miss how much it is the stabilities that allow us to even have a reference against which to perceive the flux.

This is, in fact, very unlike the wholesale mixing of information that occurs in, for example, induction between closely spaced telephone lines in the distant, but not long past, age of analog communication. It seems that perhaps the conservative nature of action-potentials in the quite ordered complex of the brain preserves important data distinctions even within the free-flowing state of the information in their associated fields. Once again it is time to re-state the probability that originally and primarily the nervous system exists for moving action-potentials from sensory organs to motor organs. And it is important for action-potentials to maintain their integrity in the appropriate nerves in order to be able to be let into the proper efferent channels should the decision (or "decision") be made to set an action going. The so-called "codings", as well as differences in nerves by type or location, are possible means for keeping action-

---

[71] I, at least, have not heard of exceptions. Biofeedback and Hindu holy men are commonly enough given as exceptions, but these are most likely cases where careful observation has been able to link conscious brain states to unconscious effects downstream of them, instead of being extensions of consciousness (except as any sort of learning extends consciousness, for its effects are thus extended).

potentials separate, thereby providing a basis against which energy/information transfers across these can have precise and meaningful effects.

There evidently are, therefore, substantial differences between the signal-garbling induction of ordinary electricity and the flexible stabilities of nerve signals. The old idea that consciousness could be a spark in a mind that is essentially just a field would seem to be simply the use of one mystery to explain another (and like many quantum explanations are said to be). This is so because, unified either by induction or not, effectively single electrical fields do not allow for the subtle constructive (and destructive) interactions of information necessary to mimic conscious processing. That being said, I would not go to any trouble to deny that some sort of internal "twinge" might occur in electro-magnetic phenomena during induction and other processes, as information and energy interact to produce what results. However, lacking any sort of continuity or meaningful reference, there appears to be little or nothing we value of consciousness in it.[72]

Emergent internalism in consciousness

Consciousness almost has to be an emergent property, even if it were just barely predicated by a dim pan-psychic awareness, that is, by a sort of internal accounting of causality, impact, or of interactions of energy and information. In this particular context it is, likely enough, worth bringing up yet again for consideration, and development, the probability that there is a kind of knowing within a system of subdivided electro-magnetism, and how well this correlates with consciousness. Changes happen in electrical fields and electrical currents, and in any changing form of energy there is, from moment to moment, the activation of potential energy (fields regularly store, in forms incorporating data, potential energy), thus the re-energizing of information. **Only internally** is this information "known", and it acts according to its own data, autonomously. How else would we describe our own experiences of consciousness?

Apparently we have to describe what happens in subdivided electro-magnetic fields as if they work internally while we experience our own consciousness, this being probably as close as we can get to demonstrating that they are the same (aside from, perhaps, some clever experiments). It is, naturally, impossible to

---

[72] Consciousness and self-consciousness are regularly confused in discussions of consciousness. I do not think of self-consciousness as being especially meaningful to discussing consciousness *per se*, yet it is one of the values in consciousness. This note is written to emphasize that what we value in consciousness is much more than self-identity, however, as many of the highest forms of consciousness are indeed accompanied by diminished self-consciousness—sublimity, beauty, and sexual pleasure are good examples.

say why we sense, perceive, and experience things consciously as we do. Let it suffice to observe that we have what seem to be widely disparate perceptions, probably relating somehow to information/energy interactions, and it is these perceptions that indicate that mental objects are typically most conscious while potentials are being activated in a mental becoming—just as we theorize (and experimentally verify) the workings of divided energy fields to do. Furthermore, it is the operation of the mind that gives us the precursors to the physical model of the internal causations and activations in electro-magnetic fields such as we find in electrical systems.[73]

Continuity in consciousness and in field states of the brain

Returning to the differences between our consciousness and cross-talk on telephone lines, though, it is worth mentioning that one great divergence of the two is the speed at which field interaction and induction happen in electricity. Even if there is a "twinge" in electrical induction, it is surely very short, and has little or no temporal continuity between inductions. Resistance would be slight, short, and not correlated with further information and the resistances against which energy, information, or both would react. That is, cross-talk has importance (or in some cases, lack thereof) in our central nervous system, while the same data would be merely white noise to any "consciousness" that might be posited in cross-inducing electricity. Chaos and white noise tend to shut down consciousness, which is why we are inclined to begin accessing stored information when we are confronted with white noise. Any form of "awareness" in inanimate, or at least non-life, situations is probably very low, if it exists at all.

In electrical loops (these require energy input to keep going, if not superconducting), however, harmonics and the like might emerge, with complex interactions being set up when different sorts of information are fed into the system. Some continuity in such an electrical system might then be possible, but actual resistance and therefore reference out of this would seem unlikely, as would any long-term stability, thus precluding the emergence of meaning. It probably is important as well that the energy input to keep electrical circuits going would tend to disturb information in the system, while by contrast, potentials in nerves simply maintain propagation of the information held in the action-potentials themselves. This allows only "intentional" (which is to say, evolutionarily selected) energy/information to propagate in the nervous system, again in all probability being quite important to a consciousness which can deal freely and unconfusedly with novel data. So not only do nerves trump electricity in the matter of stability, the freedom from disturbance by energy inputs would

---

[73] Here, too, is an important conjunction of consciousness and cognition, important because the two are experienced as being very much related.

enhance associational freedom as well. Anything else would at least dull, if not destroy, consciousness.

How might nerves allow for unconsciousness to exist?

Why, however, is consciousness apparently as restricted as it is? A good amount of information processing happens quite without our conscious knowledge, processes taking care of body equilibrium, heartbeat and the like. No doubt some induction can take place in these interactions as well. Yet it may well be minimized, and probably is not so well coordinated or permissive of much free interchange across adjacent nerves. I suspect that the conscious nervous system develops in a manner well controlled for the business of sharing and transferring energy and information inductively, adapting itself via this very means to harmonics and other coordinated transfers of energy. Unconscious nerves, by contrast, most likely minimize induction precisely to be able to produce invariant responses, and to transmit without degradation (though probably with some modification) the set of nerve firings produced by the pre-conscious, into the conscious brain. But to the extent that there is cross-talk, unconscious nerve sets may very well experience this as mere noise, and could perhaps even be able to deflect such energy/information back toward its origin.

Prevention, though, of cross-talk is the presumed first line of defense. This suggests, as kind of an aside, that myelination of nerves, while having the advantage of increasing nerve speed, may have another, and possibly more important, function of preventing cross-talk between nerves. Induction might well continue to occur at the nodes of Ranvier, the periodic gaps in the myelin sheathes, yet the appropriate arrangements of nodes likely could minimize this problem as well.

Just to add to the speculation here, this could even explain why myelination of nerves is not complete until well after the baby is born, with many nerves being non-myelinated at the time that the baby is coordinating his movements. For it could be that induction is also important in coordinating nerve development in the motor nerves, as it is hypothesized in this book to be important in coordinating information and nerve development in the brain. After the developing human has developed nerves in coordination with each other's activities, myelination can then allow finer motions by preventing unwanted movements of energy and information across separate nerves.

Specialization of nerves allows or disallows cross-talk, according to function

As speculative as this is, it makes sense because it lets inductional information transfer to occur where the nerves are developed and arranged specifically for this purpose, even as it allows the nerves that communicate this processed information to be formed specifically for accurate data transfer. Thus nerves are not forced to compromise between the best configuration for relaying information and the best configuration for processing information. The first animals presumably did have to make such a compromise, and probably did neither especially well.

Running out of the conscious processes of the brain, nerve firings hit the unconscious. Surely this is one of the great mysteries of life, that what was known becomes unknown, that even our own thoughts elude us. In spite of this, they do, and this is not the place for rhapsody, but of destroying mystery and rhapsody as much as is possible (fortunately, much mystery remains). What is quite interesting about the loss of consciousness in data sets is that there seems to be no point in time, location, or halt at which consciousness ends. Indeed, gradations of consciousness also are observed as we watch ourselves, and some who discuss consciousness write about the data that are "accessible" to consciousness.

Such a way of considering consciousness mis-characterizes what occurs in "learning", however. For although one may think again about something which was learned, and make conscious again some of what has become settled in the mind, in fact a good deal of information cannot become conscious a second time. A job such as typing becomes "ingrained", and though typing is still a conscious activity, much of the conscious information that went into learning typing really has disappeared from consciousness. How many men can only become conscious again of how a tie is tied by observing their very action in doing the task? Therefore it seems that much that is thought "accessible to consciousness", even the most "known" facts, have been lost during the process of habit-formation.

Losing conscious cognition to the non-information-processing nerves[74]

Typing and tying ties are examples of repeated behavior in which much of the information used to create the behavior is lost to consciousness. For it seems that, according to the induction hypothesis, information has shaped nerves, synapses, and perhaps some other components, to largely unconsciously route (and control the magnitude of) action-potentials from perceptions and decisions into the appropriate sets of efferent nerve signals. Consciousness continues to play a role, for each situation is unique, but mostly the nerve signals have been formed by conscious information to be routed in a manner which does not

---

[74] Obviously I am not claiming that these nerves do not process information at all, but primarily that not much cross-induction occurs, thus not a lot of information is processed.

involve significant information exchanges laterally across the sets of nerves that are recruited during such activities[75].

We can, then, gain understanding from the disappearance of data from consciousness as well as from its appearance in consciousness, for information in the consciousness seems to "program" the brain to act unconsciously in habitual activities, then it disappears. This is not to imply that the appearance of data to the consciousness does not support the idea that consciousness is simultaneous with the interaction of the information held in the differentials of nervous signals. In fact, appearance of data to the consciousness seems as if it occurs when information is in play relative to other information, while it is the persistence of conscious data which appears to be less clearly due to information interaction (although compatible with the idea)[76]. Appearance and disappearance of the contents of consciousness indicate that these correlate well with differential interactions, since consciousness largely consists in these, and the evidence of experience contends that this type of interaction (especially in regard to relational interactions) outside of the conscious is uncommon—though probably not non-existent.

Therefore myelination may help to prevent "cross-talk" and thus consciousness, although this is far from the crucial ingredient in conscious versus unconscious sections of the mind. The most important condition of consciousness seems to relate to the question of whether action-potentials can be routed and shaped primarily by nerves and synapses, or if, on the other hand, coherence and coordination of nervous signals is being effected by a subdivided electro-magnetic field which is itself existing as a unit or as subunits coordinated by energy-information interactions. For the latter to happen, potential and activation probably have to be existing in the fields according to information—this information likely being the data of form (whether quantum or not).

One thing should be noted at this point. Consciousness as context, as a sort of awareness without "awareness of...", may very well exist beyond the coordinated information and energy of the subdivided electro-magnetic field. This book's focus is on, or in truth consists of, the potential and hierarchical ordering that proceed from the energy and force arising from differentials and concentrations of energies in the electro-magnetic field. And yet it may be that

---

[75] Or it could also be that significant lateral data exchange is still effected, yet in ways that are minimally affective—harmonics, for example, might allow for some consciousness, only little "consciousness of..."

[76] To me it seems likely that persistence of conscious data beyond obvious interaction is a combination of renewing input plus the consolidation of sensorily-derived information in a context shifting in relation to it (creating a differential thereby). But this is quite speculative.

the uncoordinated field interactions around the brain's "digital" and analog processing do contribute to the apparent boundlessness of consciousness, and perhaps even provide resistance to entropic tendencies in consciousness. This is another highly speculative idea, but it seems appropriate to so speculate in the little known realm of consciousness and its place in the mind. With that having been stated, it is worth noting that such an extended consciousness may also accord with the "flux" that we seem to sense in our most subjective states.

Potentials and actualities in the electro-magnetic field, and the process of becoming

Complex hierarchical chains of mental causality and associations (which actually are essentially the same thing in this view of consciousness) are what we experience as consciousness most fully, however. What seems to matter, again, is that there be a kind of becoming, and in this case, a becoming of coordinated potentials into coordinated actions. And the latter have to become according to the former, or more like it, the two produce each other reciprocally. Little exists to create a force to shift nervous signals, except, of course, forces and the energies that these embody. I have attempted to show the plausibility that differentials within the overall force field of the brain are strongly correlated with consciousness, and also that from bare, static difference must come actual energy and form.

The further component involved in induction, and which probably turns out to play a prominent role in the binding force of consciousness, is the complex, information-rich form in which potentials (from difference, among other sources) flow into a becoming "entity" which itself eventually feeds into the action-potentials. In the visual brain this is the mental object, and it is the binding force because it in fact is the sum of an extensive yet well defined potential in a highly information-rich set of energy potentials and differences.

The becoming of potential into action presumably is most crucially the binding force in the sense that it is itself part potential energy in the shape and magnitude of the electro-magnetic force, while it is also both existing through the various differentials in the field and being defined by them. Likewise it defines and affects the existence of the differentials. This has been discussed previously. Here, though, the point is to move it deeper into the exquisite definition possible in subdivided electro-magnetic fields, to emphasize the connections across these divisions, and to underscore the coherence that would doubtless result from actualizing the potentials held in the defined field. For unlike the good objective processing to be found either prior or posterior to consciousness, within cognition and consciousness things meld, creations arise in the middle of perceptual information, and causality flows through these intermediate objects.

The brain's subdivided electro-magnetic field twists and squirms, storing energy in its sharp forms. It is unlike the system of nerves and synapses, which is surely complex enough but something that sums and scatters information. Like the magnetic coils writhing on the sun, the brain's electro-magnetic field stores and releases energy in a defined manner, and it changes itself even as it changes the flow of energy within it. What tends to be forgotten in people's models of the mind is that this surely is essential for the imagination, and for the easy compatibility of mental objects to which we are accustomed.

What size is a mental object? It tends not to be determinate, yet we typically imagine it within a certain range, at least. The "mental screen" entails that mental objects have some proportion to them. But what if we join two mental objects? It hardly matters what size anything is when visualized in the imagination, as we can fit our weapons as easily to a dinosaur as to a shrew if we imagine fighting either of these. In fact mental objects are simply fluctual, if well defined, and comparisons and contrasts are merely relative. This affords us impressive flexibility in thought, yet it is little more than the result of the fact that consciousness, and thus the objects within it, is simply relative across its scope. Conscious magnitude is largely in the strength of the sets of action-potentials. The shaping of this force is left to the fine detail and flexibility of the electro-magnetic fields as the energy follows the force lines, making them come alive and dance.

Why it is that becoming and consciousness have not typically been linked I do not know. Nothing is more essential to consciousness than becoming is, and nothing is more foreign to unconsciousness than becoming. Pre-conscious mental processing is crucially inflexible[77], as is post-consciousness (which is why our conscious decisions are effective). Unconscious drives do not cease until flexible conscious actions produce satisfaction for them[78]. Consciousness alone animates and allows shapes to become, to effect and be effected, and to pass away. This is, it would seem, because internally, consciousness is a defined potential that shifts back and forth between actualization and potential, with the information (in-formation) of both defining and controlling these transfers.

---

[77] Perhaps illusions could be argued against this—nothing could more easily tell for the inflexibility than features added to perceptions, however, whether these be anticipatory or Gestalts projected onto the visual field, for our vision can refuse us the data from the eye in favor of a very useful inflexibility in seeing.

[78] To be sure, they do "become", but probably as triggered action-potentials, thus as unchanging force.

"Permanence" and its becoming

"Reason' is what causes us to falsify the testimony of the sense. Insofar as the senses display becoming, passing away, and change, they do not lie"[79]. But what of permanence, and the logic that Nietzsche could never fully deny—and so ably used? I will admit to more permanence than Nietzsche typically did, and logic is what permits us to perceive permanence. It is a strange fact, however, that logic does indeed seem secondary, a projection and falsification of the world. This was best exemplified by the highly spiritual concepts that the Pythagoreans had of mathematics, logic, and geometry. For how could we know something that was not at all perceptible, like the Pythagorean theorem, harmonics, and geometrical proofs—or even more mysteriously, the logic that make these rationally acceptable?

In ancient times the very "permanent" and logical things made the mind reel. And Plato's dialectic with the most real—i.e. the logical realm—brought about spiritual scenarios of a becoming of the person into this reality (*Republic* and *Symposium*) and, probably later, seems to have led him to question the value of the rational (*Phaedrus*).

Plato inverted the Heraclitean flux in the *Republic*, by making the mind change to agree with the permanent, for this is the flaw in the mind's belief in permanence: that the mind has to change to come to grasp permanence and the lawful nature of logic. Because we do have logical elements in our senses, and also logical capacities beyond this (whose operations are largely non-conscious, however), the force of logic becomes felt in the flux of consciousness. Unlike other mental objects and tendencies, the rational and logical do not shift in consciousness (though some derivatives of these do), yet the consciousness itself must be shifted by logic.[80] Parmenides' ancient poem may have been highlighting just this quandary, for if the mind is thought to have the eternal judgment of logic at its disposal, how is it that the mind itself moves from not knowing "eternal" logic into the knowledge of this "permanent" rationalism?

Consciousness seems not to be directly affected by the logic produced in and carried by nerves and synapses. Neural nets are what are thought to make computations. Consciousness is affected indirectly by these computations, when logic's invariant mental effects recruit nerves to agree with it via logic's effect on the conscious fields. This, along with the rational elements inherent to vision, is probably why mathematics, and sometimes logic, can often be learned best through vision, for the derivatives of logic do appear to be produced most in the

---

[79] Nietzsche, *Twilight of the Idols* "'Reason' in Philosophy" section 2. Trans., Richard Polt, 1995.

[80] Often this shift is itself illogical, but that is not difficult to imagine from the illogical conscious mind.

consciousness, and particularly according to vision. Again, this is the triumph of the flux of consciousness, in that it can be molded and then be able to produce careless and free associations, but only according to the strict lines of causality that are found mostly if not exclusively in fields like those of electro-magnetism.

Logic's missing connection between premises and conclusions

Logic says, if...then... All that is missing from syllogisms and like forms of if-then statements is any way whatsoever to connect the two. What does connect them? Consciousness is the only reasonable candidate for this, since it has formed through experience and the movement through causal lines across associated nerve sets (associated because the fields cross) the largely harmonious sets of relations of fields and nervous signals that allow for one thing to follow another. Consciousness has also allowed the logical processes to produce indelible associations between the givens and consequents, so that we cease to be amazed at knowing discontinuous processes. Otherwise, disharmony would signal itself by a gash in the conscious flow, so that intensive consciousness could then seek to focus in on the problem in order to re-establish, through its forceful, energetic, and data-rich direction, an appropriate harmony between nervous signals and the inductions between them.

This chapter has been to a certain degree a repeat of issues thought about to some degree earlier in this book, which are again considered in order to emphasize and expand upon the importance of the becoming that happens in our consciousnesses. For this occurs contrary to logical conditions as we know these. On the other hand, the problem of induction and intersecting fields is that these are ubiquitous in both electrical phenomena and in the brain, and for anything meaningful to happen within mental activity would require the permanence that logic provides. But this logic would also have to become and would, subsequent to its becoming, affect the other sorts of coming-to-be.

Returning to the pan-psychism problem there seems to be no intrinsic problem with electrical phenomena being conscious (though this fact would be unknowable to us, unless, perhaps, we somehow could join with it and unambiguously experience something very alien). However, the very large portion of mental activity that is primarily unconscious would seem to preclude *simple* inductions and *simple* intersecting fields from being the neural correlate of consciousness by themselves (at least beyond a very dull consciousness), and that consciousness is experienced only in complex inductional data fields.

The massive coordination and interactions of energized information in consciousness

However, in the unconscious sections of neural activity there would presumably be little or no coordination of the forms and information of the

91

differentials and potentials that arise between the sets of nervous signals with the becoming of that potential within the forms of these electro-magnetic fields. More simply, in the unconscious areas, the development of data fields is not self-identical as it is in conscious fields and their self-activations via their own potential energy. And evidently it is this self-coordination of the animation of the potentials, created in the field through the activity and form of this field, which allows consciousness to know the play-out of information within itself as an internal phenomenon.[81] It bears repeating that only coherent fields can "know", or at least hold, the entirety of its causal forces and information within itself, and the same is true of consciousness. Once it becomes conscious, the information within consciousness works itself out until consciousness disappears, without the disruption of an intrusive outside monitor. Our experience is indeed that our formed thoughts develop until they reach the stage of the decision for action (motor, or perhaps mental actions), and then the consciousness of it disappears unless and until memory re-creates it again.[82]

The closed internality of conscious field activity and causality

This also yields a fine explanation for how "external" details become internal forces, and why Derrida is wrong to think that words affect each other through splitting and force (though his "trace" seems to be a try to account for more). The cuts, lines, and Gestalts that the brain constructs for our conscious disposal are resources, potentials that fluidize in the natural (or at least untamed) mind into the "painted thoughts" and glowing sparks of a Nietzsche. Deforming into causal electro-magnetic lines, they are a part of a becoming which is, indeed, heavily influenced by our experiences and values, and in turn consciousness works to re-create these. External objects affect each other by crashing about. But when their forms are delineated into the consciousness, all of the potentials of color difference, boundary, line, the various differentials that drive up our consciousness, become forces pushing causally into new mental objects (which we might create, for instance), things held fully by the conscious so that they may be incorporated into the nervous signals for action (including, of course, the creation of memories).

---

[81] Whereas unconscious interplays of the fields would be altogether too "external", too opposed and simply impacting, like it would be in the impact felt in the collision of the closed coils of magnetic fields that are of the same polarity as each other.

[82] Since this is a thorny aspect, potentially a problem, I will repeat my provisional answer, that it is possible, at least, that nervous signals formed by consciousness can revive similar consciousness, only without the richness and detail of an original produced through, for instance, visual perception.

Naturally, the argument can be made that in this scenario consciousness is never a closed "entity", and the argument would be correct. But neither is any field that is internally working out the information embodied within it, for any active field either is experiencing, or recently has experienced energy input, output, or both. The important issue is whether or not the field remains symmetrical and whole, not if it experiences gain and loss—the flux of consciousness essentially experiences both simultaneously. Asymmetry, however, is typically valued by us as evil and deformed, so the point of the natural working out of consciousness is that the drain on the energy of the conscious field be according to the forces working themselves out in a typically symmetrical fashion. The easy development of potential into actuation requires continuous internal causation in non-disrupted fields.

Only the mind can know causation and becoming, being the source of all analogous judgments of the same

There is one place in which we can know the validity and truth of causation and becoming. This place is the mind, and no matter how many errors it may make about the outside world, and even of itself, the causal links are certain (as much as we can mean anything by the term "cause"), and provide the basis and concepts we have for discovering relationships of the world and the mind. Like causality in any other field, relations are decided according to a strict conservation of energy and data, while the subdivisions of consciousness and the brain's electro-magnetic field ensure that this conservation of data and information create detailed and repeatable mental objects out of the fluctual relationships of "potential" and "actualization".

In fact I have used the terms "potential" and "actualization" as if these were really separable within the form and characteristics of the conscious electro-magnetic field, but in the case of the brain I would be inclined to say that potential and actuality are not very separate (unlike the differential forces that give rise to much of the activity of the field). "Potential" is really just a measure of the force held in a certain configuration, and while it has potency and tends to produce hierarchical effects in the less potent sections of the mental object, it is itself "actualized" and moving. This is probably fortunate for the induction hypothesis of mind, for it might be difficult to make the case for reciprocity of potential and action (and the interaction of information that goes along with it) were there a sharp distinction between the two. However this may be, the resistance and momentum of the less potent sections informs the potential as it flows into the regions of the electro-magnetic field with less potential force, while the force of actualizing potential likewise forms and energizes the information held in the more formed but less potent sections downstream.

93

Thus it is that the entirety of the mental object (and other mental processes) is energized, and the information governing the resulting shapes[83] is fluidized and interacting massively. The energy flows through this information (or more likely embodies it) in a manner reflecting all of the information reactions across the configurations of the subdivided field. Were electro-magnetic fields incapable of keeping track of these massive information transactions constantly and fully at every moment internally, the causal linkage between the activity of the field would be discontinuous with the input energy-information, and reacting to the world would be arbitrary[84]. This is entirely analogous with consciousness, for it seems to exist for little or no other purpose than to track causal information from input to output, and when the consciousness has regularly trained the nerves to act correctly, the results can be spectacularly demonstrated in athletic performances, sharp-shooting, and like activities.

So while this concept of mind does not wholly preclude non-animate, non-living minds, there is little reason to think that the right combinations of precision and complexity of interaction, coupled with the stability of carefully developed and trained (by consciousness itself) subdivisions of things such as nerves, has ever existed outside of life. Dull, uncoordinated field interactions may exist with something like awareness (I hesitate to grace it with the term "awareness", but it is all we have), but the coordinated fluidity of complex information existing in the electro-magnetic fields of the brain should probably be considered different in kind from other electro-magnetic interactions, and at the very least different to a very great degree.[85]

There apparently is a uniqueness to the self-knowing nature of consciousness[86]. For it simultaneously knows cause and effect, and how these interact (at least phenomenally—is there another way?), thus necessarily knowing itself by knowing causation in the only way possible, in a massive informational context. Even the stable parts of consciousness (from memory and logic) are in fact relative, or they could not relate to what are known to be

---

[83] And therefore the shapes of nerve signals.

[84] Obviously quantum mechanics may very well play a role in this, as aforementioned. The real issue of consciousness, however, is why such large-scale information interactions occur in our brains—after this is explained is the time to consider the deeper bases of these interactions.

[85] In fact the magnetic coils and loops of the sun may have some of the requisite complexity, continuity, and fluidity needed for consciousness, but I am guessing that it lacks the needed massive referential context that makes consciousness sharp, relatively constrained, and thus producing the potentiation of massively interacting information.

[86] This does not reach into the dullest issue of consciousness, the issue of self-consciousness. The point of the self-knowing of consciousness is that *it knows* its own actions, at least in a phenomenal manner.

relativistic parts of consciousness. Everything assimilable becomes knowable in consciousness, for the whole cannot ignore the force and form of its parts, and energy and action result from the entirety of the knowledge held in energy interactions. There was not another way for an animal evolving and developing from no knowledge to deal with the world, or at least that is how it seems to me.

Consciousness became the middle that can hold and relate knowledge in complexly changing ways. And it knows the information streaming through it because it has no way of treating data except by holding it interior to its own causal forces. It is impossible to say why consciousness comes out of this process as it is experienced, but it is possible to state that the cognitive brain has to know (or "know") information internally as well as does consciousness, and that therefore consciousness cannot be a process separate from the field holding the internal dynamics of information.

Chapter 10:

Inductions, and philosophy

Advantages of action-potentials over electricity for organisms

The original Frankenstein's monster as told by Mary Shelley became the best known cautionary tale against better living through chemistry. Later Frankensteins (to revert to vernacular designation of the monster) would, however, be animated by electricity. For from the beginning of the knowledge of electricity people have related it to life—in part because it can make muscles twitch—and also to consciousness. It turned out that the matter was not so simple as that, though, and it also happened that nervous signals were decidedly slower, energy consuming, and less transformable than electricity. But at least electrical waves were discovered fairly early in the brain.

What good were these, though? It was the slow, dull, action-potentials that seemed the real cause of nervous actions and whatever the nerves might set off. Apparently evolution had cheated us again, and we were stuck with inferior signaling and communication instead of our being electrical. Yet this picture of the nervous system has nagged my thoughts on rare occasion, because clearly electric eels, and less spectacularly, a great many other water dwelling animals, can very well make and transmit electricity *per se*. Why then did we opt for slow signals in our brains as well as the rest of our nerves? There could be a materials problem, naturally, in the use of electricity by water-logged animals such as ourselves, but this seems really not to be convincing, given the many organic insulators known to us.

Induction could really be a problem for electrical creatures, however. One might suppose that using action-potentials in nerves may well exist to prevent the induction problem, except that they plainly do not—or we would not have electrical brain waves. Nevertheless, induction may be significantly reduced by the sorts of nerves we have, so that cross-talk is made manageable by action-potentials. Whether or not this compensates for the slow rate of transmission is another issue, for nerves are very slow indeed by comparison with electrical devices. Besides, silicon machines manage to run electrical currents in close proximity.

It seems paradoxical, but in fact the "problems" of nervous signals when compared with electricity almost certainly are the advantages of animals with nerves over the disadvantaged electrical devices. The relative resistance to change effected by action-potentials allows for the development of complex informational relationships in the fields surrounding the nerves, and the slowness of the nerve signals serves to prevent these from moving too fast to be affected by the rapidly changing electro-magnetic fields that eventuate modification of the signals via induction. The brain requires too much flexibility and adaptability to be able to rely on merely one simple form of information processing. Our computers in turn rely on our consciousness to modify their operation, and likewise our nerves also need consciousness to affect (while it needs to be affected by) their operation.

Evolution of cross-talk into information-processing

One should think of the simple creatures as they developed and evolved signal-carrying cells, such as nerve cells. It seems that interference, "cross-talk", would inevitably appear between nerve cells, even if probably not to the degree that it can in electrical lines. On the one hand, the problems of interference would have to be reduced or eliminated. On the other hand, one of the ways of reducing interference would be to evolve nerve cells that responded to interference in a manner that reduced interference. And so, even in evolution's response to interference, the information in this "cross-talk" could be used to modify nerves and the signals within the nerves.

Evolution is opportunistic, however, and would not stop at utilizing the possibilities for information processing in the intersections of the electro-magnetic fields merely to reduce interference. Data interact much more finely, if somewhat less controllably, within the internal structures of fields than in the crude summations and probabilistic activations possible with synapses, including the "programmable" synapses. The other side of synapses, however, is that they are very capable at gating and allowing decisions to take place, and even of filtering the knowledge with which consciousness deals. Synapses, and the (again quite crude) logical operations, control and limit the expansive information relationships to which complex fields would otherwise tend. Evolution could not afford to pass up the opportunities that "interference" provides for complex processing, but certain mental disorders like schizophrenia may indicate the problems possible when field interactions (perhaps) become too extensive (I throw that out as something to consider, not as any sort of conclusion). There probably is a fairly delicate relationship between the desired throughput of nervous signals in the central nervous system, and the cross talk of nerves which affects this throughput.

Happily enough, as this book has tried to show, the sort of informational processing that would occur in interference and induction (i.e., fluid, continuous, and self-changing in regard to information) coincides quite nicely with what is experienced in consciousness. Any knowing (or "knowing") of the actively changing information within complex fields would essentially be entirely dependent on the (also changing) contextual information, so that an entirety has to be known at once, as happens in consciousness. We know, or think we know, how internal information would have to interact in subdivided electro-magnetic fields, and this seems to be actually based on the way in which we seem to think, so it seems difficult to find any reason to believe one to be different from another. That is to say, we probably could not differentiate what we assume would be the informational interactions within interacting electro-magnetic fields (even if we should try) from what we experience in consciousness. This means we have already set the stage to conclude that the interactions in the fields we find in the brain are the prime candidates for producing consciousness.

Unifying philosophies and psychology within the inductional model of cognition

The foregoing recapitulates the physical argument. What is fascinating to me as a student of philosophy is that this model of cognition and consciousness fits so well with the problems and concepts discussed in philosophy, as well as those in psychology. As well, it seems to point the way to the unification of disparate beliefs within at least a model of mind. Not that it necessarily tells us how fields themselves effect such a unification, rather it is a correlation and analogy of the abilities of conscious cognition with processes of the conservation of information and energy[87].

As I have stated before, I mostly came up with my own ideas about cognition and consciousness on my own in reveries on energy and entropy. Philosophy came later, but I was pleased to note that many of my thoughts had points of contact with philosophy. Derrida, for instance, manages to state essentially the obverse of what I believe to be crucial to consciousness, though unlike him, I tend to think of opposites and reversals as also readily occurring in cognition. Which is to say that I recognize that the spin-in of incidental information (information held in the complex of the differentials of nervous signals) in the brain to be mostly reversed in the spin-out of information in speech, and even that in general the spin-out would indeed be underdetermined by consciousness.

In the latter phenomenon (spin-out) I agree with Derrida in a rough sense. Derrida did good specialized work which should not be so callously dismissed as it often is, over its disagreements with science. Rather it needs integration into science and our experiences.

---

[87] Naturally there is no general, overall concern about conservation of information and energy in the brain (entropy and thermal effects are common), so that there is simply no problem that information routinely drops out as heat—I propose synapses to be primarily just such sorts of filters besides their functions in neural nets, switching, and logic. It is simply the energy and information within intersecting fields that must be conserved as long as these are in the fields themselves.

However, even though in society, and even in some of our processes of articulation, there probably is merit in Derrida's concept of how language exists and transforms itself through a constant re-cutting of words within the entire context, it is the reverse process that is the more important. Derrida's theory of the evolution of language according to its own dynamics and context (ignoring the other aspects of his ideas at present) is unsurprising in almost any development, since things generally change and become more complex through unimpeded interactions. It is the synthesis of these received words in our brains, however undetermined a synthesis it may be, that has been the true problem, and it is one of the reasons Derrida answers too little with his philosophical ponderings. For, as has been pointed out previously by his detractors, it is not clear how we could know his theory were it so.

The problem of integration is not great once the information is incorporated (integrated by that process) into a subdivided field. How could it not integrate as each field joins together to create an overall field? But as in Derridean language theory, or better to my way of thinking, Nietzschean flux, each integration is unique, unstable, and unequal with what produced it.[88] Facts and information fall into this Nietzschean, Heraclitean, or Anaximandrian flux to be unrecognizably (if very accurately) transformed into causal forms of energy. It may be that Derrida got some of his ideas about self-erasing words from this effect as well.

Fluidizing the driving differentials

Before ever reading the philosophers mentioned here, I was fascinated by the notion of what happened to data when two beautiful forms (incense smoke or the like) collided and their data-rich surfaces disappeared. What I recognized is that these data must become fluid, at least during the transition, and to re-enter and re-animate the "flux" which is forming it. What that eventuates is the destruction of that information as "object", though it is then free to *in-form* the interior, or new surfaces. Or consciously, it seems that the fluidization of information held in the differentials *in-forms* the energy fields of our minds, which we experience as consciousness. But the structure, or for Derrida the word, is indeed erased in the process (feedback lets us retrieve it from memory—*but we do have to access our memories in most cases*), soon lost to our conscious flux, which continues a while after to feed off of its causal force[89]. This partly explains how words that

---

[88] As previously indicated, some re-creations may in fact be communicated as equal in important respects—this is how we learn geometry and some other ideas. Presumably this then changes other conscious content in unequal ways.

[89] Of course more happens than just this, as deep emotional forces are often set off by words. Within this concept the triggering of emotions and the like would be from, for instance, sets of nervous signals molded and shaped by the forces and information of

disappear can nonetheless be as powerful as Gorgias stated[90], and as later psychology has affirmed.

In fact my own take on Derrida is that his philosophy must fuse back with Anaximander's, Heraclitus', Schopenhauer's, and Nietzsche's flux, but, finally, it will have to be on a physical basis. As I have noted previously, Derrida's "trace" seems to be something of a re-invention of this flux into which the definite disappears and reappears (the precedent for this is probably most easily identifiable as interpretations of the *Anaximander Fragment*), or better, certain *forms* of energy flux are erased and appear. The brain is probably the only entity that could support an energy flux like this, first of all because of the richness of information in its finely tuned divisions. And second because its nerves provide a superb method for incorporating information first into a widespread conscious electro-magnetic field, and then into the unconscious, undifferentiated (as far as the consciousness knows, that is) stream of energy in the nerves.

Freud's, then Jung's, unconscious has had little place to exist. Clearly Freud's little minds within minds has not been a great neurological success. It has, however, recommended itself to our imaginations, and depth psychology has the good fortune of coherently explaining people's actions much better than the usual conscious claims that the people doing them give. Nietzsche, especially, appears to have been excellent at figuring why humans do things, and how they subvert and change meanings. For this he invoked not only the flux (of consciousness in my view), but the possibility of changing things into opposites, at least as we interpret oppositions to be[91]. This latter is contrary to the bulk, at least, of Derrida's philosophy, and seemingly provides an important link to cognition and consciousness, and away from linguistic mechanics.

Synthesis has been one of the great philosophical problems

Hegel was, of course, the great synthesizer. Unfortunately he had no method by which such a thing could occur, but his oppositions kept synthesizing the *tertium quid.* I have proposed a couple of ways in which this could happen. These being: either by great difference inducing an electro-magnetic force which will end up flowing (supported, naturally, by electro-chemical potentials in the

---

incidentals such as words. This is how words could be "decoded" when there is no little person in our brains to do it. But then again, after conscious data have shaped nerve signals enough times, the word triggers could be much more directly routed to emotions as a learned response.

[90] In *Praise of Helen*

[91] Changing meanings and values, especially into their opposites, is a prominent theme in Nietzsche's *On the Genealogy of Morals.* Sections 9 and 10 of part one are good sources for Nietzsche's thought on it.

nerves), or by categorically different sets of nerve firings combining to make an at least substantially different third set of nerve firings (by combining, for instance, categorically different information). In this way, the induction fields allow for synthesizing both Derridean linguistics into consciousness (which Derrida did not do as far as I know), as well as the Heraclitean, Hegelian types of oppositions.[92] Harmonics would be yet another sort of "opposition" which can be produced via an unconscious induction, although *consciousness of* harmonics is probably held in the more usual manner.

Hegelian synthesis does at least point up the grave problem of change and movement within our toolkit of rationalism. This has been a huge problem at least since Parmenides in his poem conflated the problem of becoming with the becoming of judgment itself, properly refusing to split off change in the mind from change in the world. Logically, the Parmenidian problem probably has no solution, but fortunately empirical observation makes us aware of flux, something that is recognized by the mind probably because, as was further discussed, the mind itself has a great deal of flux in it.

Internally we experience the flux consciously, externally we find electro-magnetic fields that must have an internal flux, as empirical science tells us. It is this flux which allows us the recognition of change as the perceptual information obtained about external flux melds with the flux in the mind. This creates the sort of identity of non-equal things sought by Hegel, and denied by Nietzsche, that is, it allows for synthesis. And it is this flux that allows us to know the (relatively) permanent criteria for judgment, for only the changing entity could come to know the comparatively permanent. Actually, it so happens that consciousness really does have to be a flux in order to come to an initial knowledge of anything, so it is fortunate that the best candidate for the neural correlate of consciousness is the synthesizing potential of interacting, data-rich, electro-magnetic fields.

Qualia as possible energy-inducing differentials, driving the flux in part

As a model, at least, this version of what consciousness is holds the promise of bringing together and illuminating a number of the problems in philosophy and psychology. Of course a number of questions remain, and further questions will also be raised (if not, it would not be a productive idea). The biggest problem is probably unanswerable—why do we experience consciousness, especially qualia, as we do? Why would internal energies working through information "illuminate" our data-complexes as they do? Some discussion of the matter follows in the appendix, yet as we in fact begin knowing through this

---

[92] Certainly this does not allow for the extensive oppositional syntheses of Hegel, however.

experience, and it is thus important, we probably should nibble around the edges of it and discover whether or not some ideas are plausible.

I do consider the flux of consciousness to be more primary than I do the question of qualia. As I presume Nietzsche would, I observe that the qualia are in flux and capable of being energized as are the non-qualia data and emotions. Furthermore, the manner in which two different colors in close proximity can provoke what seems to be a mental potential seems to point to an energetic factor at least related to qualia. Indeed, it was by looking at roses of somehow "oppositional" colors that mostly gave me the idea of conscious potentiation through energy differentials, for at least that was how I experienced it at the time. Does the sight of pink and orange (or Rio Sambo) roses force an inductive flow in the brain?

The brain's *tertium quid* as the model for perceived syntheses

It would seem so, and it also appears probable that the same inductive force was necessary to model the idea of an electric current being induced by similar poles of magnets moving past one another. For without the brain being able to produce a *tertium quid* as a concept, the production of a new form of energy from moving "opposites" would have to be considered as "magical", or simply as an empirical fact. Even if electricity is to God, for instance, merely an empirical fact, we understand it through our mental models of transformation. It is an odd circle that comes out of our models of electricity. For we understand electricity through our conscious experience (rightly or wrongly—but necessarily), we measure electrical activity in the brain, and then it seems almost inevitable that we would non-logically, but through the sense of identity that we project onto electricity, recognize that electro-magnetic phenomenon are also identical with consciousness. Qualia seem to be able to act much like our designations of plus and minus in this regard (or not, in some cases—clashing colors are merely judged to be "bad"), so it seems the phenomena of qualia are at least subsumable under the energetics of electro-magnetism.

Summary

I have noted that electricity has been associated off and on with consciousness since we became highly aware of electricity. This tendency is sometimes reflected in our language ("spark of an idea"), and of course is a typical model used to explain nervous impulses. What has been lacking as far as I know is a reasonable explanation of how consciousness and cognition could work in the brain, and I have herein sought to give a simple conceptual framework for something which is no doubt a good deal more complicated than I have realized. But I believe that I have shown that it has broad-based explanatory power, the ability to bring vexingly incompatible phenomena and philosophies at least closer together.

It could be that this is an overly abbreviated account and consideration of model of consciousness I am proposing. I do have time-constraint issues pushing for a short book, and generally prefer thinking about the subject to writing it. Still, I believe that the biggest reason I have decided on a small book is that it is difficult to convince the intended audience to read a graduate student's work—understandably the supply exceeds demand. It seems best to write something not too off-putting, and not something that relies on the effort needed to read it in order to convince people. Repetition has been used, but I thought it likely that I would have to repeat concepts that are somewhat unfamiliar. Additionally, much of the repetition has been due to the attempt to come at the matter in several different ways, to expand on a phenomenon when the approach changes. This concept is meant to unify the several basic means for understanding the world, and, I hope, to partly bridge the chasm between analytic and continental philosophy.[93]

I have not focused greatly on possible problems with this idea, for it is my responsibility to, at least at first, state the positive case for it. Nor have I made much use of references, because consciousness is a fundamental problem which I believe has simply not been adequately considered, in my reading of it in any case.

If this work stands I shall miss having quite so much mystery surrounding consciousness, but the soft intensity the colors of roses in the rain remains, I hope untouched by the words that allow it to correlate with our rational world. I have wondered if consciousness should be explained at all, but because people insist on making the brain out to be a "computer" or the like, and because rationalism and surfaces dominate our lives in ever increasing amounts, an explanation such as this is unlikely to threaten our spiritual side. It may be that it could even open possibilities to people who think that what we now have are incomplete but mostly satisfactory views of the brain and mind.

Therefore I attempt to cast this out into the critical gaze of philosophers and others. It has been my pleasure to think about thought, and we shall see how a different context might transform the products of a conscious forging.

---

[93] Nietzsche especially, since I believe he is one of the most subjectively self-knowing persons, at least among those making it into the canon.

Appendix

The qualia problem

I have suggested that we seem to sense the causal force in sensation as the electro-magnetic fields interact, based on a very good reason—this is how we determine causality experientially both in perceptions and in whatever we propose and purpose. And I have further surmised that qualia act in energetic ways, most obviously when differential seems to induce a force (naturally this may be only in certain sensing modes). So there are plausible suggestions about how fields may produce changes that are apparently internally sensed in consciousness.

I think, though, that this should be explored further, or in any event I have some thoughts on it that I believe should be presented both for this book's hypothesis and for the sake of thought on qualia itself. This was originally to be discussed in a chapter, yet it did not seem to fit well in a case for flux and energy/information interactions. I wanted to present the reasons for thinking that qualia were not the primary issue before showing that if the interacting fields correlated well with consciousness, qualia might at least agree reasonably well with these. Now is also the time to admit that qualia remain problematic enough. Perhaps continuing mystery is not unpleasing, but remaining difficulties are surely caveats for the hypothesis as well.

Nevertheless, some of the qualia most associated with objectivity, namely color, have possible associations beyond those mentioned in the last chapter that seem to agree well with field interaction being at least heavily involved in our consciousness of color. The production of new colors through blending optic signals seems quite congruent with the production of the *tertium quid* from dissimilar colors, although it is quite likely to occur not in consciousness, but prior to it.

The disappearance of color into the neutral signal of white

What is most interesting to me, however, is that, when in the consciousness or otherwise, colors seem very much to be relative to each other. In fact, because an "equal" mix of the primary colors creates white in the mind, apparently qualia *per se* can just as easily disappear from consciousness as appear. While it may not be within the consciousness that this happens, it does call into question the primacy of qualia in consciousness in that qualia are configured to blend to create the colorlessness of white. Perhaps it is even that colors are only very accidentally what they are to our consciousness (or at least the colors after the first evolved one would be accidental), because they must be of such a form and informational content that their combination will make white.

An objection could be raised, objecting that white and black are indeed qualia as are the primary and some of the "secondary" colors, but I do not think so. In effect black and white are binary signals, white filling in the "mental screen", black leaving a blank by contrast. This is not to say that black is not represented in the consciousness in a positive manner, however. The rods, which detect black and white signals, seem even to yield a black and white as relative, naturally producing shades of gray. It would appear likely that from very early on, and probably from the beginning of sight itself, contrasts were what mattered, because indeed it is the changes across the field of vision are what produce pictures, in our experience.

One assumes that probably one color arose later on, well after the rods gave creatures black and white vision. It may not have been just one in fact, and that one color could only exist if another did as well, since they are relative. However I would think it more likely that only one would arise at the beginning, due to the complexity of evolving even one "color" of cones, and the even more impressive brain circuitry to deal with it. What probably is inescapable is that it would have to exist relative to the sight we have from the presumably original rods with their black and white signals.

Fitting the "first color" into black and white vision

To touch on Edwin Land's retinex theory of color perception, a color like red would, if it were the first evolved color, have to fit relatively into the "brightness scale" of our black and white vision. Land had it that colors are relative to red, but red could not have evolved first as an adequate medium for conveying information if black and white were not also related in a similar way (or vice-versa—actually none of the colors, nor black and white, are absolute) to red. For if the things that looked red at dusk looked white at noon, constancy of perception would have been seriously compromised.

Who knows what the first color looked like, or even if it looked like a color at all? What is clear is that as later primary color cones evolved, their signals had to "add up" with the first color to produce colorlessness, white. Originally a locational signal, white did not initially have a relation to color (that is, not before there was color), and probably would not have been thought a quale if color had not evolved—shape, form, line, and possibly shading might have been thought of as the qualia of sight. Or if white is a quale, surely it must at the least be considered to be significantly different from the color qualia.

So it is hard to say why the first color looked like it did (whatever that was). Later colors may not entirely have an explanation for how we experience them either, but one factor in how they were perceived would surely be that they would have to combine with the other colors so that in the correct proportion they ceased to be qualia—or at least not qualia of the same kind. I do not believe that this relates greatly to consciousness—I do consider most color mixing to be preconscious[94], but even this caveat serves to point out that qualia do not exist exclusively in consciousness, rather being the bearers of information which may be "interpreted" not only in consciousness but even in pre-consciousness.

The incidental nature of color qualia

I believe that it is safe enough to suppose for the time being that qualia are not the central fact of consciousness, however much these enrich consciousness. When color perception is readily destroyed for the consciousness of "white", at the very least this means that the more evolved qualia are thereby pre-empted. And even were white to be considered a quale, at the very least several qualia have their potential destroyed in order to represent information with one simple quale. But as implied above, I do not think white *per se* is much of a quale, more just a "colorless" signal of stimulation in the visual field whose qualia in black and white would be mere incidentals from the contrasts of light and dark.

Colors, on the other hand, are definitely qualia, but are frequently subject to the mix of the other colors, and to black and white. In the consciousness these have differential potential, and it is in this way that the information embodied in them reacts and controls nerve firings. Colors are usually preserved to show up in consciousness for that reason, but if the information is as easily collapsed into the "code" of white, there is no need or effort to preserve the qualia as potentially generated by the eye's cones.

Losing qualia in order to preserve the energy balance of consciousness

The fact that there is not preservation of qualia—indeed, apparently deliberate loss of qualia in the pre-conscious—makes it look unlikely that qualia should be considered as at the basis of consciousness. The pre-conscious mind selects and combines information to the right form and mix for the consciousness to deal with the data it receives—one reason for combining colors into other colors or into white. For white objects would otherwise over-stimulate the conscious process when viewed by cones instead of by rods, as these would then glow in the several primary colors of the brain. So the force of qualia is adjusted prior to the (relatively) free associations that occur in the conscious processing, in order that differential forces should not be created artificially by the visual

---

[94] Blending of pixels and the like are probably in or near the conscious, as are the fluorescent effects of the impressionists, but colors appear to be mostly separate in the conscious, supplying potential and difference to drive consciousness. This presumably is what happens in the fluorescent effect of impressionistic paintings.

distinctions made according to the wavelength reflectivity of our surrounding world.

Thus, even in the instance of color qualia, credible arguments can be made both for the non-primacy of qualia within consciousness, and for a pre-conscious treatment of color in order to fit the differential forces driving conscious cognition. Because of the importance of qualia to perception and cognition, it was important that these be plausibly compatible with the primacy of the flux of force in consciousness. In any event it manages to suggest a more dynamic consideration of qualia, and I hope of consciousness as well.

Glen Davidson

About the Author

The author is a philosopher with a strong background in science. I took a pre-med humanities course for a BA, and philosophy for MA. I intend to study for my doctorate, probably using this book for my doctoral thesis. More importantly, I have long studied on my own the sciences, philosophical matters, and the humanistic areas, especially for the sake of my interest of consciousness, beauty, and what we might be able to know about ourselves.

Crucial to the book and its value is that I have spent some years without school, or establishment work, dabbling with art, nature, and especially writing, thinking my own thoughts and not those of others. Most books have little reason to be written, for the authors are simply re-doing old ideas, if perhaps developing these ideas a bit. That is why we need the Ralph Waldo Emersons, or Nietzsches, people who did not stay forever tied to academia and the system. At present they are lauded for that, while anyone today who is outside the system still is given little consideration. Yet it is still we who have the experiences to think new thoughts.

So I have combined a wide-ranging education with a dip into my own unconscious mind. Oddly, this seems like it would be essential for consciousness study, yet I have read little about consciousness by anyone who has experienced the range of consciousness. The New Age, telepathy and ESP types do not count, since romantic sentimentality is hardly an asset in considering consciousness. While I do not claim to be Emerson, or better, Nietzsche, reincarnated, I can say that I know about the unconscious resources of the mind all the while having a deep respect for science. I believe that consciousness has to be explicable, though not reducible, to both scientific explanation and to the intense symbolism of unconscious imagery.

This is why I wrote the book, to consider both the "spiritual" and the scientific aspects of consciousness, where these converge and where they diverge. And in fact this is truly the decisive factor behind writing the book, to work out ideas I had of consciousness in an integrated manner. I knew that publishing would be difficult, for publishers do not like what makes life worth living, edging toward the spectacular sights surrounding the black vagueness of the void. I publish this way because I do not trust them, and take measures to prevent them from possibly ripping me off. If it is read, that is good, however it is also up to you.

www.ingramcontent.com/pod-product-compliance
Lightning Source LLC
Chambersburg PA
CBHW052245290526
45785CB00016B/1397